My First Hundred Years

Donald R. Fletcher

My First Hundred Years

A Life on Three Continents

DONALD R. FLETCHER

RESOURCE *Publications* · Eugene, Oregon

MY FIRST HUNDRED YEARS
A Life on Three Continents

Copyright © 2019 Donald R. Fletcher. All rights reserved. Except for brief quotations in critical publications or reviews, no part of this book may be reproduced in any manner without prior written permission from the publisher. Write: Permissions, Wipf and Stock Publishers, 199 W. 8th Ave., Suite 3, Eugene, OR 97401.

Resource Publications
An Imprint of Wipf and Stock Publishers
199 W. 8th Ave., Suite 3
Eugene, OR 97401

www.wipfandstock.com

PAPERBACK ISBN: 978-1-5326-9645-9
HARDCOVER ISBN: 978-1-5326-9646-6
EBOOK ISBN: 978-1-5326-9647-3

Manufactured in the U.S.A.   10/08/19

To Martha,

beloved partner for seventy-two years,

who added so much to my life.

Contents

List of Illustrations | ix
Acknowledgments | xi
Preface | xiii

1 "Look to the Rock" | 1
2 Foreigners in a Familiar Land | 5
3 Voyage of the *S. S. Sphinx* and Beyond | 16
4 Needing to Be Brave in a New World | 24
5 Fear and Love of the Sea | 31
6 Rolling for Eight Days and Nights | 36
7 "In Praise of Old Nassau" | 46
8 Beer Jackets and Pine Logs | 52
9 Martha | 60
10 Medellín and Mountains of the Moon | 71
11 Going North | 76
12 "Oasis of the Soul" | 81
13 Communism and a Lecture on Melville | 88
14 A Play with a Purpose and Leaving Home | 91
15 Caribbean Travel and a Front-Lawn Wedding | 99
16 A Gospel Parable and a Department to Chair | 106
17 A Last Supper and a Madonna by Raphael | 114
18 "Have You Thought About High School Teaching?" | 121

19 Unexpected Call | 127

20 The Gradual, Total Eclipse | 134

21 Three-Digit Milestone | 146

Illustrations | 153
Other Works by Donald R. Fletcher | 163

Illustrations

Frontispiece. Donald R. Fletcher | 11

Photo 01. Family portrait with Don, age one: Archibald G. and Jessie Rodgers Fletcher and children Archie, Don, and Elsie, 1920 | 153

Photo 02. Senior year at Pyongyang Foreign School, 1935 | 154

Photo 03. Martha and Don, dressed for a formal concert at Westminster Choir College, 1943 | 155

Photo 04. Studio portrait of Don and Martha as new missionaries, 1945 | 156

Photo 05. Don leading a youth group on the Antofagasta shore, 1950 | 156

Photo 06. In the pulpit of the Iglesia Presbiteriana Cristo Rey, Antofagasta, 1953 | 157

Photo 07. Portrait of Don, age 42, 1961 | 158

Photo 08. Martha and Don in Cherry Hill, 1987 | 159

Photo 09. Family celebration of Martha's and Don's 50th Wedding Anniversary, 1992 | 160

Photo 10. The family at Martha's Memorial Service, 2015 | 160

Photo 11. Portrait of Don, age 97, 2016 | 161

Photo 12. Don with his six children, celebrating his 100th birthday, 2019 | 161

Photo 13. Don still preaching at age 100, 2019 | 162

Acknowledgments

ANY LIFE-STORY, PARTICULARLY ONE that has spanned a century, shows an interweaving of many influences and many personalities. It is impossible for me to acknowledge my debt to all who cast their shadows, short and long, across the pages of this story.

In the writing of it, though, I wish to recognize that it was my daughter Sylvia who proposed and encouraged the project, from beginning to completion, giving hours and whole days to the detailed preparation of the entire manuscript. Others of the six children who came to fill the home and busy life of my wife, Martha, and me have helped, supplying insights and recollections.

Martha preceded me, in late 2014, passing the boundary of this life, and I gladly dedicate this book to her.

For timely help, overall and with practical details, I appreciate the skill and counsel of my literary consultant and valued friend Roger Williams of Washington, DC. And, finally, I am glad to have again, for this present volume, the courteous and effective support of Wipf and Stock Publishers.

Donald R. Fletcher
Lions Gate, Voorhees, NJ
July 2019

Preface

THERE IT WAS AGAIN, that poignant, haunting melody, as my classical music program was signing off. I found out later that the melody was Fauré's Pavane. For now, it moved among the shadows, the low light of my hospital room in late evening. And it brought back once more, for no specific reason, that distinct, remembered scene.

I was in northern Chile, in some dusty town of what they call the *Norte Chico* (Little North). We had been riding south all day and into the night on the tawny, washboard ribbon of road across the desert *pampa*, several young Chileans, and I at the wheel. We needed lodging and a few hours of sleep. We spotted a two-story inn on the dark, unpaved street. The double leaves of a heavy wooden door were closed tight. As Fauré's music swelled, I was seeing again how one of the young men struck a match and we tried to find how the door was barred, as our knocking and beating on it had brought no response.

That was all—the detached, remembered scene formed and faded each night, along with that poignant sign-off melody, in the shadows beyond my bed. Why that particular inn door, a fragment of a mostly forgotten journey? It wasn't part of a memorable adventure, nor of some critical happening; just a single, isolated picture that the brain brought back in emotive detail, when that music infused my imagination.

Yes, my physical energy in the hospital was very low. I'd been through surgery for superficial bladder cancer; then the cancer was back, more invasively. With the help of my family, I'd consulted several options, settling on a radical, reconstructive procedure offered by a team at the Department of Urology of Rutgers University's School of Medicine, and the Robert Wood Johnson Hospital in New Brunswick, New Jersey. It was a long surgery, some twelve hours, involving clearing out all possible organs that could be, or become, cancerous; then construction of a "neo-bladder" out of a

Preface

segment of intestine, completely connected, to function almost normally as a urinary bladder. No need for an external pouch, to be tended to for the rest of my life.

The surgeons were hesitant, as Dr. Robert Weiss, the one with whom I continued to consult, later acknowledged. The oldest patient on whom they had performed their experimental operation was sixty-five, and I was eighty.

"But he's in excellent health," Dr. Weiss had affirmed; and so they agreed, with my concurrence, to go ahead.

The surgery was successful, and recovery seemed, at first, to be progressing well. But when it was time for me to begin to supplement the IV with soft nourishment by mouth, a tray came up to my room. I tried the food and vomited. Anything I attempted to swallow was thrown out violently.

Long days of observation followed. Each morning the house doctor, very pleasant, originally from India, came by on his rounds, trailed by a queue of students because this was a teaching hospital. Each day he questioned me, almost coaxingly. Had I at least passed a little gas. No, nothing. There was an intestinal blockage, and it was total.

The IV was my lifeline—my only lifeline. Strength began to ebb. The various tubes used to keep me drained were closely monitored. The IV could sustain life, but not strength, which was fading. My family was there, different members by turns. They needed to keep me moving, to get out of bed and walk, trailing my tubes, which were secured on a steel pole that I pushed along. But the effort was formidable.

My daughter Sylvia, especially, urged and insisted that I make it out of the room and down the corridor. When she let me stop and turn back, I saw the door to my room. It looked far away, at an impossible distance. How could I get to it? How could I finally just get on my bed again?

Dr. Weiss came to see me, almost four weeks after the surgery. The surgical team had concluded that another operation was necessary. Was I willing?

"Yes, yes. Let's do it." I was ready for some action, any action, to make progress.

That was how, in a late night of that second recuperation, my spirit turned hopeful again. There would be years, yet. And if I had the time, I would write.

Preface

It was a prayer to my God. I wasn't asking for a bargain, a *quid pro quo*: do this for me, and I will do that for You. It was just that I began to feel that there were thoughts and ideas that I needed to put into words—books, even, that I needed to work at writing.

"If I can have fifteen years," I thought "I'll use them to write."

That second surgery cleared the blockage. I was able to eat. Strength began to return, and after the expected two weeks—making mine a total of forty-four days in the hospital—I went home, carefully. I still trailed two of my tubes, and had a wide, deep incision that needed to be monitored and dressed by a visiting nurse, while it healed from the inside out.

But in time the first book took shape. I had begun it as a long narrative poem, an imaginative telling of how the beautiful New Testament Gospel of Luke came to be written. I recast it and rounded it out, in prose, giving it the title *I, Lukas, Wrote the Book*.

Now I have had, by God's transcendent grace, not fifteen but twenty years of good health, and eight books have been published. This is my ninth.

1

"Look to the Rock"

> Look to the rock from which you were hewn,
> And to the quarry from which you were dug
>
> (Isaiah 51:1 NRSV)

SO COUNSELS THE PROPHET in the Hebrew Scriptures. The rock from which I was hewn was the staunch and spare tradition of Scottish Presbyterian faith, as exemplified by my dad, Archibald G. Fletcher, MD, and, in softer form, my mother, Jessie Rodgers Fletcher. Arch Fletcher's forebears had migrated, several generations earlier, from Scotland to Canada; those of Jessie Rodgers, from Scottish Northern Ireland to Philadelphia. Now these two young people, coming from very different settings, had enlisted individually with the Board of Foreign Missions of the Presbyterian Church in the U.S.A. and had been sent to Korea.

This was in the second decade of the 1900s. Japan had annexed Korea, as the ancient Korean kingdom collapsed; but in terms of Christian mission enterprise, the people of Korea were proving to be remarkably ready and responsive, and Japan remained open to and accepting of Western influence.

Arch and Jessie, both in their late twenties, were part of a thrust of recruits eager to learn the language and customs and to adapt to the needs of the Korean people. After several years, they found themselves together in Taegu (also spelled Daegu), a provincial capital in the warm southern part of the Korean Peninsula. Arch, a Canadian farm boy from Ontario, was assigned to the medical work in Taegu, while Jessie, a Philadelphia girl, was there provisionally, helping with a large gathering of Korean women.

Different though they were, Jessie and Arch quickly found that they enjoyed one another's company. It was spring, and several bewitching May evenings were enough for a very brief courtship. They each knew who they were, and now knew that they were in love. The proper mission and civil authorities were consulted, and within a short time they were married.

The major social adjustment fell to Jessie. She was now the doctor's wife, making a home just up the hill from the hospital, such as it was. And very soon she was pregnant. Baby Elsie, my sister, arrived the following May, and a year later, in August of 1917, my brother, Archie (Arch Jr.). My appearance came in January of 1919, but not in Taegu. That is another story.

*****

"Dr. Adams, please, come quickly. Arch needs you."

The Rev. Dr. James Adams, veteran senior missionary, lived next door to the doctor's house. He had wakened to a timid but urgent knocking on his bedroom window. When he got it open, he made out the figure below, just recognizable in the first glimmer of daylight.

"Why, Jessie, is that you?"

"Yes, yes! Please hurry!"

Dr. Adams found his shoes and a wrap against the chill of late winter. As he and Jessie crossed to her house, she told him, in brief snatches, what had happened. Arch had been working all day—seeing outpatients through the morning and performing one surgery after another in an afternoon that stretched into evening. He got home too exhausted to eat dinner; just fell in to bed. Now, only a short while ago, he woke her.

"Get me a basin, quick!"

When she brought it, he coughed up a torrent of bright red blood. At first, she didn't dare leave him; but she had to have help.

The basin was still there; the blood darker now.

"Yes, Jessie, you did the right thing."

Taking charge, Dr. Adams, first thing in the morning had a telegram sent to the main mission hospital in Seoul. Arch's father and his eldest brother had both died of tuberculosis. The significance of the pulmonary hemorrhage was clear. He dared not make even a modest exertion, while the family packed for the earliest passage available across the Pacific to the United States.

Arch had to watch helplessly, while Jessie shouldered the whole burden of preparing to leave, with no assurance that they would ever return. There was no treatment, yet, for tuberculosis. The "cure" was rest, with plenty of fresh air. When the family was back, finally, in the eastern US, Arch would be spending long months in a sanitarium at Saranac Lake, New York, while Jessie and the children lived with her parents just outside of Philadelphia.

It was a stressful time, more so because Jessie was pregnant again. How vast was her relief when Arch wrote, in October, that he was soon to be released from the sanitarium. The Pennsylvania Medical Missionary Society had several cottages, on the Jersey shore, in the town of Ventnor, and he had secured the use of one of them for the family.

To Jessie it seemed dream-like to stand in front of that white clapboard, two-story cottage in the late October sunlight, with Arch beside her, looking quite fit now, holding toddler Archie by the hand, while Elsie ran ahead excitedly to try the door. This would be home—their first family home in the United States.

The cottage had a screened porch on the second floor, where Arch, obedient to his "cure," could sleep in the fresh air. It was certainly fresh on that cold night of January 6, 1919, but Arch was not sleeping. In a second-floor bedroom, lights were burning past midnight. It was now the seventh. Jessie was in labor, and Arch was the physician-in-attendance.

Why not use the hospital in nearby Atlantic City? Arch had investigated the cost, which he himself would have to pay. He had delivered both my sister and my brother in Taegu; now this third baby, who would complete the family. He wrote his decision to his doctor brother Gordon, in Orchard, Nebraska, and Gordon promptly sent a complete obstetrical kit—including a surgical gown and gloves, and the latest drug in use to ease delivery. Arch was equipped—plus, he had at his side a registered nurse, a missionary wife also on furlough, who served in Siam (now Thailand).

Happily, the birth went well. Around 2:30 a.m. I entered the world. Elsie and Archie were sound asleep, which also was well. Our parents were both in their early thirties when they were married; so, by their choice, we three had come along quickly. In fact, for four months each year, from my birthday, January 7, to Elsie's, May 2, our ages would always be consecutive—like three, two, one. That gave Mother a handful, when we were small.

She came to love that Ventnor cottage, though, as winter turned to spring and then summer. Her life was taken up with her new baby and the other two children. Arch, always eager to make the best of any opportunity, now turned his medical focus to tuberculosis. The disease was widespread in Korea. He attached himself to an x-ray specialist in Philadelphia, learning all that he could.

The Board of Foreign Missions in New York supported those efforts, anxious to see him fully restored and purposeful before sending the family back to Korea. That meant that I was a curly-headed one-and-a-half-year-old when our family of five was on a ship crossing the Pacific to Japan, then by ferry to Pusan, Korea, and finally by train to Taegu.

2

Foreigners in a Familiar Land

It was a different world that opened to my early childhood perception and acceptance. Our family was still the firm center. Dad was with us on work days, morning and evening, and for a short while around noon, when he came home for lunch. Leaving the lunch table, he would sit for a few minutes in his large Morris chair and relax, taking off his glasses. But if he dozed and they slipped from his fingers, he would get up with a start and quickly be out the front door and down the path toward the hospital buildings. Mother (she didn't like "Mama," "Mommy," or "Mom") was in charge of the household, which came to include Kang Si, our cook, and Pak, our "outsideman." We didn't have an "ammah" for child care, as some families did. Mother chose to take care of us herself.

I became aware that our house was at one end of a compound, which was the mission's Taegu Station, built along the crest of a low hill that overlooked the city. Around the compound there was a mud-brick wall topped by clay tiles. If I were helped to the top of the wall, I could look out across a sea of straw-thatched houses built close together, with a few streets along which there were some tile-roofed shops or more affluent homes. That was Taegu in the 1920s—not the modern city of almost three million that it is today.

In my early world there were people, including my family, who were not like most of the rest. We were "foreigners." The word had no hostile overtone in my child-world. In fact, it had a comfortable feel, because that was our identity—who we were. Around us, other people were Koreans, except for the occasional Japanese official of some sort. When Dad, for a rare outing, took us downtown in the family Ford touring car, children might gather around to gaze at us as a curiosity. That was not pleasant. We found that a solution was to pick out one of *them* and point and giggle, which tended to disperse the onlookers.

Why didn't our parents—and most missionary parents at that time—encourage us to mingle and play with the children around us? There were small graves in some mission cemeteries to answer that. This was Korea of some ninety years ago. Not only were the familiar childhood diseases prevalent, but also more ominous ones—dysentery, typhus fever, even leprosy. In his practice, our dad was encountering these every day.

For a halcyon time, while I was small, Taegu Station had quite a few children. The "big kids," mostly, went off to an English-language boarding school in Pyongyang. But there were enough younger ones, for a time, that their parents put together to employ a teacher for a one-room school. Mrs. Gordon's School was a mysterious, near-legendary place to me, even in its final year, when Mother felt ready to start Elsie and Archie together there. I have a blurred recollection of being taken to the school for a visit once, near the end of the school day. Here was a new thing: familiar forms and faces sitting in rows—my own siblings among them—all with quiet, serious looks, paying attention while this one adult talked to them and some took turns answering her. How special it would be, I thought, to be part of that.

But that all changed. The Korea mission sometimes moved its personnel, according to its developing program. It happened that a couple of the families with early-school age children were transferred from Taegu. Mrs. Gordon's School was disbanded.

*****

It was about this time that something memorable happened. Mother, exceptionally, was away in Andong, gone to comfort a new widow who had lost her husband to malaria. Dad encouraged her to go, saying we would be fine for a few days.

It was winter—cold enough, even in southern Korea, that our house had a furnace in the basement for warm-air, radiant heating. From the furnace, a sheet-metal flu pipe passed up through the first-floor and second-floor hallways and into the attic, where it bent and entered a brick chimney.

On this morning we three children were at breakfast with Dad. Still in our pajamas, we had kicked off our slippers under the table, as we liked to do, when suddenly the sewing-woman, who was upstairs, came rushing, almost falling, down the staircase. Her face was full of fear and she could hardly speak. As she frantically waved her hands, Dad went bounding up the stairs. Archie followed, and Elsie dared to go half way up; but I stayed at the bottom.

Archie told us later that when he got to the stair landing and looked up, he saw little tongues of flame licking down around the hall flu pipe, where it passed through its asbestos-insulated opening into the attic. When Dad opened the door, the attic stairway was full of fire.

Immediately, all was commotion. We three ran out into the yard, forgetting our slippers. Looking up, I saw flames shooting out of the attic windows. Fortunately for us, at the mission academy for boys, built on a low hill a quarter-mile away, the students were just gathering. The quick-thinking principal, catching sight of our smoke and flames, called together a group of the oldest boys and sent them over, on the run, to help.

They rushed in and began to haul out whatever could be saved. Upstairs, they pulled clothes out of closets and dropped them out windows to others below, who carried them to safety. Downstairs there was a piano. It wasn't ours; our parents were taking care of it while its owners were on furlough. This was one of the old-fashioned "player pianos," with its mechanism of perforated paper rolls coupled with foot pedals to create a suction that worked the keys. The whole thing was ponderously heavy; but somehow these schoolboys picked it up and carried it outside.

Most of this I had to learn afterward, from the telling and re-telling. To our chagrin, our neighbors' daughter—one of the "big kids," who was in her early teens—corralled us, all three, and shut us in one of their bedrooms with the blinds drawn. She was sure that if we watched our home burning we would be emotionally scarred for life. But how frustrating, more for Elsie and Archie than for me, that we couldn't see the excitement—such a rare happening in our world!

I later learned, from a more adult perspective, more of the details—such as how the city fire company arrived but could do little. The weak water pressure in our compound—built on a hill—left their hoses useless. Nothing could be done to damp its flames, the house blazed like a torch for the whole city to see.

What about Mother, as all of this was happening? There was no telephone line to Andong, no means of emergency communication. The telegraph was all, and it was cumbersome, with text very limited. Besides,

Mother was expected home that same day, and she would be unreachable as she traveled by jitney over seventy miles of rutted roads. The winter daylight was already waning when at last the jitney—a Model T Ford chassis fitted with three crowded seats—entered Taegu and Mother began to look for familiar signs.

They came into the wide street that she knew, but as she looked up, she thought, "That's strange. I don't remember an abandoned building there." Above her, on the hill, there were some empty brick walls—no roof, and windows that were just holes through which she could see the evening sky.

Then suddenly it hit her. "That's no abandoned building. That's our house!"

The jitney honked its way, agonizingly slow. It seemed to take forever to reach the corner and turn toward the hospital. But there, before she could move to climb out, a figure came running. It was the sewing-woman. She had been waiting and watching, anticipating how Mother might feel.

"Lady, lady," she called, "the Doctor is safe, and all the children! It's all right!"

Mother hugged her, which was unusual in Korean custom. Gradually, as Dad came out to meet her and as she at last reached us at the house where our family would provisionally be lodged, she heard the whole story.

We had a new outsideman, who had been instructed how to light the furnace on a cold morning. He would use the small branches of dry pine needles that were effective in getting the molded balls of soft coal to start burning. But this furnace was large, as everything that these foreigners had seemed to be. He would pack in an extra amount of the resinous pine branches.

When he struck his match, the pine ignited with a whoosh. The almost-instant blaze leaped up the chimney. Flames, perhaps igniting some soot on the way, shot up the sheet-metal flu pipe, all the way to where it bent in the attic, with such heat that the pipe gave way. Quickly, stored items caught fire, with a sound that startled the sewing-woman, who then was terrified to see those small flames licking down around the flu pipe.

The Japanese police arrested the hapless outsideman. They needed someone to blame and to arrest and would have clapped him into their feared prison; but Dad argued his case—he was simply trying to do his job very well. Reluctantly, they let him go.

Were we children scarred for life? Not so. But Mother told me later that, at times that winter and the next, when she would lift the lid of the pot-bellied stove in our bedroom, letting a few flickers light the ceiling, I would get tearful and want to hold on to her. That much stayed with me.

*****

In Taegu, after some families with children were moved and Mrs. Gordon's school could no longer be maintained, Mother turned to an educational resource used by US expatriated families across the world—the excellent Calvert School in Baltimore, Maryland. We three became familiar with its label on printed materials and complete supplies, down to pencils and erasers. Mother kept Elsie and Archie in one grade and started me in the next. I would listen in, avidly, on their lessons.

We were assigned to teachers in the far-off Calvert School. Some of our completed tests and important papers were sent there; but boat mail was slow—no trans-Pacific airmail yet—so such contact was tenuous. Mother was our resource for learning, bolstered by the superb Calvert School materials, including fine reproductions of classic art and architecture.

There were fewer children, now, in Taegu Station. Two or three older ones, like our neighbors' daughter, Harriet, were away at boarding school in Pyongyang or in college back in the US. Our age group numbered four—we three Fletchers and Huldah Blair. Huldah had two older sisters; but the age gap was wide. She was now the only Blair child living at home.

The Blairs' house was the last one at the other end of the compound from ours. As we four found ourselves left to our own resources outside of home-school time, Elsie, Archie, and I became familiar with the trek along the clay road, the whole length of the compound ridge, to play with Huldah. Mother kept our school work to week-day mornings; but sometimes, when we turned up at Blairs' in the afternoon, we might be told that Huldah, who was also in Calvert School, wouldn't be out for an hour or two that day because she was behind in her lessons.

Let me add here an interesting aside. Huldah was just a couple of months older than Archie. Both were born at home in Taegu in the midsummer heat of 1917. One morning, Mother, her own pregnancy far advanced, had gone to help with Susie Blair's new baby when, on the way home, she felt the first signs that Archie was on the way. So those two—indeed, we four—grew up together and went off to college. Archie studied medicine, enlisted in the US Army, and was in Germany with the Medical Corp during the occupation after World War II; while Huldah, now an RN, served in a mission hospital in Costa Rica.

Their contact during and after college had been only casual. But now a warm correspondence developed, and soon they realized—by mail—that they were in love. That led to a long and happy marriage; a medical missionary career in India, during which five sons were born; and a serene retirement in Southern California.

As children in Taegu, we four played games, inventing new ones as we could. The side yard of our house was gravel, just a thin layer over rock. It was on the sunny side of the building, and Mother was determined to grow some flowers. The outsideman went to work with a pick, chipping at the sedimentary rock a short while each day, until there was a rectangular basin deep enough to hold the soil for a small flower plot.

Then we took over. In the basement we found half of a packing case for an upright piano. The size was just right, to cover that flower-bed excavation. We also found some rice straw to make it more comfortable inside. One could wriggle through an opening we left at one end, and a few—if not all four—of us could squeeze inside our shadowy "barrow." It was a special place. A point of protocol established that anyone, on entering, must be chewing one of the faintly sweetish stalks of the rice straw.

In those brief childhood years, I had no awareness of choices our parents were making. On the table there was always hot food for dinner. I didn't think about where it came from. I did know that Pak, the outsideman, had a bicycle on which he would bring back purchases from the market, such as a pair of chickens tied together at the legs and slung over the handlebars.

The trouble, it seemed, was that those chickens had spent their short lives scratching and foraging for food, which meant that they were lean and tough. Dad, the former farm boy, found an answer. He directed the construction of a lath-and-wire-netting pen in our backyard, complete with an enclosed hen house with a roost and nests. We would have occasional fresh eggs, plus a well-fed chicken for the table.

The experiment succeeded so well that, in time, there were broods of fluffy chicks—all quite fascinating for us children. But then the trouble began. There was commotion in the hen house at night—loud squawking—and in the morning some baby chicks were gone. Arming himself with sticks of firewood, Dad positioned himself at an upstairs window, from which he could let fly at any marauding animal.

That helped for a while. Then, one night, the squawking was unusually loud and frantic. Dad hurled his stock of firewood, aiming as close to the chicken pen as he dared, and eventually there was silence; but in the morning his favorite brooding hen was bloody all around her head, and only two of her chicks were left. The afternoon before, while we were playing in the backyard, we thought we glimpsed a slim, brown shadow that disappeared behind the wood pile.

Dad brought a trap from the hospital. It had an end compartment, where he could shut in a live chicken. Then there was a larger compartment with a treadle and a trap door. When an animal entered there and stepped on the treadle, the door would drop shut behind it.

Dad set the trap inside the chicken pen, and it worked! In the morning there was a very frightened chicken in the end compartment and, shut in next to it, a small, snarling, unbelievably ferocious animal—a weasel. We tried to feed the weasel bits of raw meat through the wire of its cage, but it ignored the food, its ferocity intact. After only two days, the wild creature died.

I haven't mentioned Tootsie, our small dog. She was of an uncertain ancestry, white, with some brown markings, cute and lively, with a suggestion of Pekingese. Dad had spoken for her from a friend and colleague in another mission station, where the family dog had produced a litter. The doctor friend came to us by train. It was winter, and he brought the pup in his overcoat pocket, keeping her quiet by letting her suck on his fingers. We named her Tootsie, from a popular song of the 1920s, and she became our constant companion.

About the weasel, though, she was sensibly wary. She barked at it in its cage, ruffling her neck fur and showing her teeth, but not coming very close. After the weasel died, and Dad found a taxidermist downtown, who stuffed it in a life-like pose, mounting it on a wooden stand, just a sniff of it would send Tootie (we usually dropped the "s") into a paroxysm of scrambling and barking. After some months, moths got into the weasel's fur, where it was put away while we were gone for the summer. It had to be disposed of; but we kept the end of its tail, and for a long time after—when we children were older, and Tootie, too—producing that tip of tail and giving her a sniff would set her to racing wildly around, as if the snarling creature were right there again.

*****

In Taegu there were other experiences—trivial childhood happenings—but such as left impressions on memory that are still there, after some ninety years. In two of these, it was an unexpected act of kindness that made the impression.

Archie and I were getting interested in kite flying, which at the time constituted almost a major sport in our region of Korea. Of a long spring or summer evening, if there was a stiff breeze, we could perhaps perch on the top of our back wall and see the kite masters in an open street below. There might be two of them, standing thirty or forty feet apart, each surrounded by his group of cheering onlookers. All would have their eyes fixed on a patch of sky where two square kites were battling, climbing and diving, or moving laterally, as their expert handlers worked the thin kite strings. Those strings hung, in an inverted arc, from the reels of the handlers, up and away through the evening air, to their tiny, darting squares fifty or eighty yards away.

The last five yards or so of each string had been dipped in glue and then passed through powdered glass. If the glass-treated string could be made to cross the taut string of the other kite, then given a sawing motion, it might cut that other string and send the opponent's kite floating helplessly away.

Archie and I watched such contests with fascination. Once or twice we were able to recover from one of the trees on our compound a hapless kite that had been cut away. But the memory I want to share was of nothing that grand. It was early in our kiting experience. I had made a very small kite, following the very maneuverable Korean design, and Archie had built a similar, but larger one. It was a bright, breezy Saturday morning when we boldly took our kites outside the compound wall, near its far end, to a place where the land fell away in a wide, grassy slope. There were already other boys there with their kites—not foreigners like us, of course.

My small kite would only spin erratically in the breeze. Archie took off running with his, and I was left with this useless thing on the end of the strong thread I was using as a kite string. Then one of the boys, about my age, came up to me. Smiling, he took from a pocket in his short, Korean cloth-jacket some scraps of paper and, in a heavier, folded piece, a lump of rice-flour paste. He put together a paper tail and pasted it to the bottom corner of my kite. Smiling again, he had me try it, and the little kite took to the air, holding quite steady for its small size. I thanked him, with the phrases of Korean that I knew, little thinking that more than ninety years later, as I write, his warm, shy smile and his finger rubbing the flour paste— the spontaneous kindness of his gesture—would still be with me.

Another memory that my brain still holds brings in our dad. The scene is the lower corner of our yard—again, a late spring evening. The family Model T Ford is there, with the engine hood lifted off. There is some problem, and Dad is conferring with a couple of men about it. In the era of this memory, trained auto mechanics were not available as yet in Korea—just those who had been learning by experience. Dad was a person of caution and persistence, and in this case, it showed in a very long discussion.

Archie and I had been standing by. Whether he understood anything of the conversation, I don't know. I did not; but as long as he stayed, I would stay, too. What persists in my memory, after Archie had found some place to sit, is that Dad went around behind the car and brought an empty gasoline can—one of the five-gallon cans that were the only way, then, of transporting the fuel. He placed the can kindly for me to sit on it.

I was used to following Archie's lead, and to his getting attention in any sort of manly, adult-type matters; so, Dad's thoughtfulness toward me made an impression, deep enough for that memory to live on. Archie, as I've mentioned before, was only a year and five months older than I, but much of the time I was definitely the "kid brother." He was more outgoing, more sociable, and he proved to be much more athletic. It was exactly right that he should be named A.G. Junior, and that, as I said above, he should follow Dad into medicine and a career as a missionary doctor.

Many years later, I am remembering a photo of him and Dad. Both are wearing appropriate academic regalia. As a Canadian and still a British subject, Dad had qualified to be inducted as a Fellow of the Royal College of Surgeons. Now he was a US citizen, and he and Archie, in the same ceremony, were both being named Fellows of the American College of Surgeons.

Growing up, I was more domestic than Archie. I enjoyed being where Mother was—listening intently when she read, although infrequently, from one of the American poets, perhaps Whittier or Longfellow. I remember that once I suggested to her that Archie and I were like the Biblical twins Esau and Jacob—Esau the hunter and outdoorsman, Jacob a man of the tents. Mother didn't like the comparison and immediately discounted it. Probably she was thinking of the conflict between the brothers, after Jacob tricked their aged father into bestowing on him the paternal blessing of the firstborn. I gathered very clearly that there should be no more talk about Esau and Jacob.

In effect, I always felt close to Archie, respecting his strong points. We roomed together through boarding school, and also at Princeton, when I joined him there. I made an unsuccessful effort at soccer as a freshman, but Archie was on the varsity team and before he finished was named All-Eastern halfback.

I gladly remember one of the last times we had together, just the two of us. He was a first-year medical student at Columbia in New York City. He invited me for a weekend visit, squeezing a cot into his tiny dormitory room. I enjoyed sharing, at night, his view of lights festooning the George Washington Bridge. And I recall, some five years later, when Martha and I were newlyweds, how he visited us and laid on our dining room table the returned ring of his first engagement, which had been broken off.

*****

For many of us there come moments of a personal epiphany—whether in childhood or later in life—when our spirit spreads its wings, testing the air. I carry from my childhood, even now, a clear impression of such an experience.

Members of Taegu Station used to gather on Sunday afternoons for an English-language service. Most of its members were involved elsewhere on Sunday morning, and perhaps evening as well, in services in Korean. The afternoon gathering was an opportunity for sharing and mutual uplift in the language and traditions that were our own. I was still very young, not mindful of much of this; but one Sunday Mother sang a solo, choosing a hymn of very personal faith and devotion. She was not a trained singer but had a pleasant voice and was just taking her turn.

A day or two later I was playing alone in our front yard near sunset. We had a Weeping Willow tree there, and the low, golden sunlight came slanting through its trailing branches, which were just beginning to sprout their tender leaves. I stood still, with the melody of that hymn and my mother's voice filling my head. Even to a child, the situation, the sound, the whole late-sunlit scene were powerfully, transcendently poignant. There was an awareness of Spirit, of Reality quite beyond; but for that moment, intersecting my simple, day-to-day reality.

I was perhaps six or seven at the time. I had no language to express such an epiphany. I still don't, really, but am profoundly grateful for that unspoken Word that let me spread my spirit's childhood wings. That was God, touching me.

Of other childhood epiphanies, I am remembering just two. For one of them I was probably a bit younger, because there were more children on the compound, including a couple of "big kids." They had organized a game, maybe some sort of war game. There was a patch of tall grass, and I was told that I was to lie there. I must remain very still—just lie there until someone came for me. Perhaps I was supposed to be one of the wounded; I don't know.

The voices moved away, and everything grew still. Where I lay, I could look up, between some stems of tall grass, into the sky—a deep, tranquil sky of mid-afternoon. There was a small, white cloud moving slowly across it, and then another. I had never before felt how deep the sky is. I was lifted out of myself, out of my world, received and absorbed into that serene vastness.

How did the experience end? Did someone finally come for me? Apparently, the bigger kids had forgotten this wounded casualty. As I remember, I at last got up and went looking for them.

The other childhood epiphany I am calling up takes me to a different venue—Sorai Beach, a missionary resort on the northwestern coast of Korea, where our family had a summer cottage. The cottage stood on a bluff, with a zigzag path that made a steep descent to rocks and a bit of stony beach below. We mostly went to the community beach, a beautiful stretch of sand at a ten-minute walk; but this day Archie, Elsie, and I had taken the steep path down to explore the rocks. I was probably seven or eight.

We found a place where the tide had left a small pool in a deep cleft of rock. That pool was a microcosm of the sea world, with green moss on the rock, a few strands of seaweed—even a couple of sand crabs scuttling nearby—while the warm sun lit up its clean water. I was fascinated by this miniature seascape. Then I happened to look up. My gaze took in the zigzag path up the bluff. At the top was a shape, one corner of our cottage roof thrusting out and beyond it, the crystalline space of sky. For that moment, it wasn't sky. It was Beyond—Spirit—what is ineffable. I had—and have—no words for it. My spirit felt, for that brief, timeless moment, its reality.

3

Voyage of the *S. S. Sphinx* and Beyond

IN KOREA, AS I was growing up, the term of service for Presbyterian missionaries was seven years, followed by a one-year furlough in the United States to be used for rest and refreshing. The furlough was also for promoting the mission cause—visiting churches, renewing contacts, spreading information, and inspiring a positive response.

Because Dad's medical leave extended the furlough during which I was born, he and Mother offered to extend their succeeding term to eight years. Having returned to Korea in 1920, they would leave in 1928. Dad, who always had a plan in mind, had learned that our family of five could make the journey "by the ports" for not much more than going straight across the Pacific and the continental United States. "By the ports" meant boarding in Japan a ship that would cruise down the coast of China, around the Malay Peninsula, across the Indian Ocean, up through the Red Sea and Suez Canal and across the Mediterranean; then, by a different vessel and after travel in Europe, across the Atlantic to New York.

There would be stops in numerous fascinating ports along the way, as well as opportunities for land excursions. We children would be a bit young to get the full benefit—Elsie just twelve, Archie close to eleven, and I nine-and-a-half. But the next furlough would find all three of us in college.

Dad secured passage on the *S.S. Sphinx*, a ship of the French line *Messageries Maritimes*. It was my good fortune that, in Hong Kong, a British family with a son named David came on board. Now I had a playmate who was just my age. There were quite a few other children, particularly after the ship made port in Saigon, then the capital of French Indo-China. But they all spoke French and couldn't understand us; nor we, them.

David and I learned our way around the ship. As she cruised into equatorial waters, canvas awnings were stretched above the open deck aft, where we Second-Class passengers could stroll or sit. David and I discovered that we could walk and even bounce on the taut canvas, although as our coal-burning vessel steamed along and soot gathered on the awning, we heard loud objections from below when some of it sifted through. That was French that we could understand, without knowing the words.

Another time, in our games we made us a flag. We went to the extreme aft rail of the ship, to the short flag pole, and started to haul down the red-white-and-blue of the French national flag so that we could raise our own. A sailor saw us and came swiftly to push us aside. We got the gist well enough, through his shower of French expletives, as he angrily restored the Tricolor of France to its rightful place.

There was no air-conditioning as yet—the *Sphinx* steamed along with portholes open. One evening, at the early Children's Dinner, I was seated below one of them when a freak wave struck the ship's side and the frothy crest surged through the porthole, drenching me, to the stifled merriment of several nearby tables. I felt deeply chagrined, as Elsie took me back to our cabin to get changed. It was a long voyage—though longer, I'm sure, for our parents than for us three. But eventually we reached Suez, at the southern end of the Suez Canal, and there left our ship, to take a train to Cairo.

I won't catalog all of our travels. In retrospect, I admire how Dad and Mother were able to stretch what they had saved over the seven or eight years, so that our family of five could manage modest accommodations and a considerable amount of tourism. In Egypt it was just Cairo and its environs—then on to the Holy Land, British-controlled Palestine. Our parents were people of devout faith, well-versed in the Gospel story. To be in Jerusalem, to visit Bethlehem, the Jordan River, Nazareth and the Sea of Galilee—these places, and the sites said to be linked with the life of Jesus, all were meaningful to them, and perhaps somewhat so to my siblings.

For me, it was just new and different to be moving constantly from place to place, even if the sites seemed much the same. I do remember one encounter with a shepherd boy who showed us his skill with a Palestinian sling—how he put a stone in the pouch fitted with two long thongs. Holding both of them in one hand, he set the stone pouch to whirling around his head at a dizzying speed, until, with incredible timing, he released one thong, letting fly with the stone straight at his target, which it hit with a frightening crack. This was a sight for a nine-year-old tourist to remember.

Another memory, both of sight and sensation, was sinking up to my neck in clear, cool water of the Sea of Galilee. Dad had found a small inn on the lakeshore that had a sheltered cove at one side. We had no bathing suits in our luggage; but Mother decided that the cove was private enough for us to go swimming in our underwear. The day was hot, and it did feel wonderful, just to settle into that limpid, refreshing water. There were smooth stones on the bottom, and when I raised my eyes, the far shore lifted and wavered a little in the hot air on that tranquil lake surface. It was, for a mature Christian, a holy shrine, as it would be for me later in life. For then, it was just a completely delightful setting to experience.

After Palestine we returned to Suez, at the northern end of the canal, to take another ship of the French line. Through some cross-up, there was no reservation for the Fletchers. Dad, the experienced negotiator, argued our case and got all five of us quartered on hospital beds in the single, quite large room that was the medical department's isolation ward. This served very well for the voyage across the Mediterranean to Marseilles, France, our ship's home port. What I remember from that voyage is Stromboli, the isolated island that is just a volcanic cone thrust out of the sea, off the north coast of Sicily.

We passed near enough to see tiny houses clustered on one slope, beneath a small cloud of smoke that hovered over the crest. A good while later, as our ship steamed away and the summer dusk was gathering, I could gaze aft and glimpse, on the underside of the volcano's plume, a ruddy tinge from the burning lava in its cone. The far, shadowy glow still lives in my brain's memory.

That memory retains little else from the rest of our family's journey to the United States. Our funds would not reach for spending much time in Europe. I have only a blurred recollection of the gloom of some lofty cathedral naves, of flights of stone steps, and the hallways and casements of museums. What I do recall, in Paris, was the purchase, for Archie and me, of navy-blue serge suits with short pants, and a British-style cap to complete them. The cap I remember, because I put mine down in the Louvre, at the feet of the Dying Gladiator (a.k.a. Dying Gaul), making Dad return with me to hunt until we found it. That gladiator is one statue I didn't forget, as I also remember the crisp feel of the serge suit—an extraordinary and extravagant purchase, it seemed to me.

Voyage of the *S. S. Sphinx* and Beyond

Apparently, time and money did not allow for any tourism in the United Kingdom. We crossed the Channel only to proceed directly to Southampton, to board ship for New York City.

*****

In Princeton, New Jersey, on Alexander Street, stands a discreetly handsome, three-story building, Payne Hall, which houses twelve apartments designated, preferentially, for missionary families on furlough. It was a natural fit for us. We were given the use of Apartment D-3, on the third floor at one end of the building. From its balcony we could look down at traffic—still a novelty to us children, used to the isolated mission compound in Taegu—and across the street to the campus of Princeton Theological Seminary, the chief Presbyterian school training men for the ministry (no women graduates in those days).

The summer was past, public school was the new venture. The Calvert School course, with which we had been home-schooled in Taegu, was an accelerated program designed to prepare a student for high school in six years, rather than eight. When we left Taegu, Elsie and Archie were finishing Calvert's fifth year, and I was half-way through fourth. The public school in Princeton placed them in seventh grade and me in sixth.

The rather long walk to and from school took us through a central part of Princeton University's campus. My siblings' junior high school dismissed its students later than my elementary school did. Doing the return walk alone, I could loiter, to admire carved tigers on a stone gateway and absorb something of the neo-Gothic feel of what was then the university's Lower Campus. All of this was new, as so much else about suburban life in the United States in that year spanning 1928–1929.

In the Payne Hall apartments, there was another family on furlough, missionaries to some country in Southeast Asia, I think, who had two daughters. Jean, between Elsie and Archie in age, was vivacious and inventive. I found her fascinating, although beyond me. She had a talent for impersonating adults, including some public figures of the time. I, of course, knew nothing about public figures in America, but joined eagerly in the applause when Jean was imitating their characteristics and foibles. Jean devised grown-up games that Elsie and Archie seemed to understand, and I wanted to play them, too.

On the other hand, there was Julia, Jean's younger sister. Julia was perhaps a little younger than I. I have just one recollection of the two of us—a game she and I were playing on a warm day, venturing to use an open, grassy slope beside one of the seminary buildings. I think it was some kind of war game, and I was a wounded casualty; we were of the post-World War I generation. What I have in memory, once more, is an impression of sun, of closeness to earth and grass, and of a wide, cloud-sailed sky beyond the spire on that seminary building. I was a bit uncomfortable, though, with the game, feeling that it was childish.

Two other recollections may show my bashful eagerness to fit into this world full of other children, after the isolation of our recent childhood in the Taegu Station compound. One of these involved the elementary school, which was on Nassau Street. There were some rather tough kids, of Irish parentage, who occasionally took notice of a student as obviously different as I was. And in our grade, there was also a boy who was quite chubby, also a target for them. In one recess period, when we were all in the school yard, the Irish kids brought the two of us together, trying to get us into a fist fight. We didn't want to fight, nor had any reason to, but were being boisterously egged on and didn't want to seem cowardly or weak. Quickly, a ring of onlookers gathered around, which made us even more conscious of needing to fight acceptably.

Of course, a teacher intervened, and within a day or two, I was with Mother in the principal's office. The principal had an idea that she could get the other boy and me to have some training with proper boxing gloves by the school's athletic director and put on an exhibition match to demonstrate our real manliness. It was an exotic idea, and nothing came of it. Yet I do give that principal credit—at this long remove—for wishing to enhance our self-esteem and to show up those bullying toughies.

There were playful, prankish moments as winter gave way to spring on the university campus, with large, delicately transient magnolia blooms here and there. On a warm Saturday we found that from our third-floor balcony we could take aim with a water pistol at cars passing below with convertible roofs folded back. And in the long evenings, joining with other kids as dusk was coming on, we could run and hide and call each other "out," among the shadowy houses. It was a good time, but brief.

As soon as school was over, our family needed to start on a deliberate trip back to Korea. The deliberate part was because Dad again had a plan. With some gifts he had carefully gathered, he had bought a Silver Anniversary Buick—the beautiful 1929 model. Was this extravagant? In appearance, it wasn't exactly a "missionary" car. Dad's reasoning was that a Ford could not be expected to hold up on Korea's rutted roads for seven or eight years, until the next furlough. Perhaps the heavier, more solidly built Buick might do so. His next project was to equip this car with a carrier in front for a large picnic cooler and a rack on one side for a tent and some sleeping bags. His plan was that we would camp our way across the United States, from east to west, saving on lodging, while we enjoyed the countryside.

Along the Lincoln Highway, as on other principal routes, there were occasional tourist camps that might offer an area for tents, plus a cluster of cabins, plain and spare, with men's and women's facilities in a separate structure. Dad's Buick was adapted so that the back of the front seat folded down to form a bed of a sort.

On our first night on the road, after a late start and a short run, we found a place to camp. It was dusk already and the sky looked threatening, as Dad and Archie pitched the tent. Then we boys bedded down in it, while Elsie insisted on squeezing in with Mother and Dad in the car bed. That was a wise choice, because rain came on. The tent was on a slight slope, and there was no ditch around it to divert the water that flowed in, sopping Archie and me. Mother was resourceful; but I don't recall how she coped with helping us get through the night.

The next day brought us to Pittsburgh. We might possibly have gone a little further, but it was Saturday. My parents' conservative Presbyterian tradition—that rock from which I was hewn—based their observance of the Christian Sunday on the Biblical commandment and ordinances of the Sabbath. Therefore, they would not travel on Sunday. We would find a suitable campsite in the environs of the city, to rest there until Monday morning.

Our camping location was pleasant enough, at first; but then we began to realize that Pittsburgh, at that date, was a coal city. The gritty dust seeped into everything. We were glad to pack up and roll westward on Monday. And it should be recorded, although perhaps at Dad's chagrin, that from here on, for most of our overnights, the camping gear stayed packed up while we used tourist cabins.

An intermediate destination was Orchard, in northeastern Nebraska. This was to visit Dad's family, which was easy, because his three brothers and families all lived in Orchard, and his one sister and her husband lived in Clearwater, not many miles away. When both of Dad's parents died, and the children, now grown, decided to sell the family farm in Ontario, Canada, each took his share and went his way. Tom, the eldest, moved to Nebraska, where he settled and prospered in business in Orchard. Dad, Gordon, and Dave all chose to study medicine, and the latter two set up a joint practice in Orchard, which they continued for the rest of their lives. To complete the picture, the only sister, Olive, married a doctor and settled in Clearwater.

In Orchard I was happy to find that Gordon's youngest child, Bruce, was a boy almost my age. For the few days of our visit Bruce became Archie's and my companion, showing us many things about the half-rural life of the small town. Bruce had a Daisy air rifle, a "BB" gun that used compressed air to fire the little lead pellets. This seemed to me an intriguing, grown-up-style toy.

When we were ready to leave, Bruce and his parents insisted that I should have the Daisy. They could easily get another, and they knew that, with the strict Japanese custom officials and the import duty charged, there was no way that I could order one and have it sent to Korea. I had that air rifle in Taegu for years. Archie and I used it to shoot at tin cans and such. We took some shots at birds, but, while abundant, they proved to be very small and quick-moving targets. Once we did score a hit on a crow, but the bird just flapped its wing, knocking the pellet from its feathers, and flew away.

Our next westward stopover was Yellowstone National Park. There were wonderful sights—cascades of the Yellowstone River, brilliant hues in steaming pools of the Geyser Basin, and, of course, an eruption of Old Faithful. But to me, the most memorable experience was sitting in an arc of benches at Old Faithful Inn near dusk and watching, at a safe distance, while bears came from the woods to explore a garbage heap, and a park ranger regaled us with anecdotes, his comrade astride a horse nearby, cradling a rifle for security.

I enjoyed the jokes and anecdotes so much that I retained them and would retell them with gusto to any adult audience that might be assembled with Mother and Dad. In spite of my shy nature, I always, even from an early age, took pleasure in that kind of "public" speaking.

A final experience, from our family return to Korea that year, came with the ship's brief layover in Hawaii. We went to the famed beach at Waikiki, and Dad shared a rare outing with Archie and me, renting surfboards. Naturally, we couldn't ride the surf, so we lay on the boards and paddled, kicking also with our feet. It was fun, and the water was sparklingly beautiful. We stayed out in the sun much longer than we should have, Dad included.

The result—a burn by that Hawaiian sun, the most severe sunburn any of us three had ever experienced. We could only lie face down on our bunks afterward, writhing as Mother went from one to another, anointing us with cold cream as gently as she could. We had no other emollient available. She did observe that Dad, as a physician, should have considered the risk of exposure to that unforgiving, subtropical sun.

About the return to Taegu I have little recollection. It was a blurring blend—familiar sights renewed, but in a different light, while our home bustled with preparations for a new chapter in the lives of Elsie, Archie, and me. We would be off, within a crowded pair of weeks, for Pyongyang, some four hundred miles to the north, to the mission-supported, English-language Pyongyang Foreign School. The quiet life of the small, home-schooled world in Taegu was gone. Ahead was a whole new scene: boarding school with other children ranging all the way from upper-elementary age to high school seniors.

The prospect—all unknown—was exciting, bewildering, unnerving. Elsie and Archie seemed to regard it as something wonderful, so I tried to feel the same. When the time came that Mother and Dad took us to the station and we got on a train, leaving them there, I tried to enter into the excitement; but inside I was already torn by the loss of what I was leaving behind, wrestling with what this drastic change would bring.

4

Needing to Be Brave in a New World

FROM THE LANDING THERE were four more steps to upstairs, four more of these padded steps. As I climbed them, I looked up. There was a hallway, and at the end of it an open door.

There she was! That had to be right! I knew that skirt! The rest of her was hidden by the doorway, the way she was sitting. I could just see the ankle-length skirt and her feet; but I knew the skirt.

It looked far away, infinitely far. Could I reach it? Could I get to it? I took quick steps. She heard me, and I could see her face, smiling at me. The skirt—I was close to it—and seeing her now, as she was, above it. That, just that, was what mattered. The whole scene is still vivid to me: how I felt on Mother's first visit.

"Why, Don, dear!" she was saying. "I didn't expect you to come over from the dormitory."

I wasn't saying anything. I wasn't crying, either. I was just pressing close to her, close to that skirt that had been so impossibly far away. Mother had come up to see us after our first couple of months at Pyongyang Foreign School. Perhaps Elsie had written her that I was homesick, although I tried not to let it show. Now her visit gave me a tremulous happiness; but the visit was short. When she left, a wave of homesickness washed over me again.

It was a wave, though, and waves pass. Although Elsie and Archie were making their own friends, I had them with me in the dormitory. The dorm, at that time, was just one building, two-and-a-half stories, housing forty or fifty of us in rooms on the second floor and in large open areas on the third, up under the sweep of the heavy, clay-tiled roof. Secure doors on each of the upper floors separated them in two halves, girls on one side and boys on the other. The ground floor was for the kitchen, dining room, living room, and the matron's small bedroom and bath; the laundry was in the basement.

I lacked the outgoing nature of my siblings, I nonetheless experienced pleasurable times. I'm remembering one spring evening of that first year. I was behind the dorm, on a steep bank where flowering weeds grew among some trees. I had found a slender, pliable stick, which was my sword. I was wielding it in knightly combat, beheading weeds of my enemies, when Ben, one of the high school boys, came up where I was—a unique event for me.

Ben joined in, had me describe my combat and shared in my make-believe world. After a while, he said, "Yonder, there is a damsel who is waiting for me. You will excuse me, Sir Knight, as I go to meet her!"

I have never forgotten Ben's kindness to a younger, solitary boy on that spring evening. Possibly Elsie put him up to it. If so, I never knew.

A new thing for me in dorm life was that there were many girls—older as well as of my age group. Of course, I didn't speak to them; but there were two whom I selected as the most beautiful and bewitching. The older and taller one, whose blonde hair hung in waves, I privately called the "Queen," while the other one, was "Princess." Only later did I learn that these two, whose real names were Marilyn and Rachel, were sisters.

One day in late spring, after dinner, our housemother called us together in the living room. She told us that Marilyn was sick, very sick, and had been taken to the hospital. She led us in a fervent prayer for Marilyn's recovery and told us also to pray in our rooms.

The next day, the principal gathered all of us, those from seventh grade on up, in the Assembly Hall, to tell us about Marilyn—that it was meningitis. The doctors were doing what they could, but the fever was very strong. Marilyn and Rachel's parents would be coming from Chefoo, in China, as soon as they could.

He invited us to kneel at our benches, and anyone who wished to, one by one, to lead us in prayer. I was in awe, hearing the emotional outpouring of my schoolmates—particularly one of the senior boys, who began to pray and broke down, while several senior girls were sobbing.

That evening word was passed that Marilyn had died. The light of my Queen had gone out. I didn't cry, as that senior boy had done. I asked Elsie to let me, and I went to climb that bank behind the dorm, finding an open place where I could sit still for a while, letting my feelings sink into place before I went up to the third floor, where Archie and I had our beds, side by side.

The next year I was in eighth grade and more confident. In our small school at that time, seventh and eighth grades were in one classroom on the ground floor. (Elsie and Archie had moved upstairs to the high school.) I began to speak up more and take initiative; and I began to notice girls of my own age. One of them was Beatrice—called Bea. Dark haired, with eyes that could flash, she was bright and a leader. In class I was sometimes in competition with her. That winter, though, there was one rare and memorable experience.

Behind the high ground on which our school, dormitory, and a number of missionary homes were built, the land fell away to a wide, level valley. There were mud-walled, thatch-roofed houses with rice paddies, and among them, a small river, the Pothong (POH-tong). The large Taetong River flowed past Pyongyang, far away on the other side of the city, as it was then.

In the cold north Korean winter that I'm writing about, both rivers were frozen over. There came, one Saturday, an evening of clear sky and full moon. Some of the older kids, and some adventurous teachers, arranged a new and one-time-only event for all of us who wanted to join in: a moonlight skate on the Pothong. Elsie, Archie, and I went, and in the excited group gathered in light and shadows at the river's edge, putting on our skates, I saw that Bea was there.

The better skaters took off quickly, Archie among them. The rest of us did some circles, getting the feel of the ice. Then I saw that some of the older kids were pairing off, skating side-by-side and matching strokes, while they crossed arms, holding hands, left with left and right with right. I went up to Bea and asked if she'd like to try it.

We weren't skilled on skates but found that it went quite well. We followed those who were skating up the river, away from houses and people, but always we stayed near others of our group who were passing in one direction or the other. Bea had a fur-trimmed jacket, and mittens with fur on the back. She was also a "dormite" (as we called students living in the dorm), whose parents were in China, an area near Korea, and this was real fur.

I got to know those mittens well, as we kept skating together a long time. Bea seemed to like it, and I knew that I did. We went quite far up the small river, skirting places where the current had made the ice rough. It was hard to spot and negotiate them in the moonlight, but that made the adventure more enjoyable. The emotion of that night is with me yet, after these many decades.

As I said, this moonlight skate on the Pothong happened just once; but there were also walks home from study hall at night, sometimes with Bea. We dormites had study hall each school-day evening, all of us in seventh grade and above. There were two forty-five-minute periods, with the lower three grades staying for just one period and the upper three for both.

It certainly wasn't far from study hall to dorm—maybe eighty or a hundred yards; but we didn't have to walk fast, and it provided a brief, sentimental interlude. It turned out that Johnny, a classmate who also fancied being with Bea, began to try to get in ahead of me some evenings. She seemed to have the same smile for both of us, and to prefer, quite often, to walk with her girlfriends instead.

As we moved up the ladder in school there were other emotional interests, but Beatrice was always there in my thought, at least in the background. Finally, in my senior year she was totally eclipsed by my infatuation with Edna.

Edna's family was in Seoul, her father a missionary doctor like mine. There was a small English-language school in Seoul, but Edna had apparently been getting behind academically, so her family decided to send her to PYFS. I was ahead in school, fifteen and beginning my senior year. Edna, a freshman, was, I think, fourteen, or near to that. Physically, she was precocious, with the full figure of a girl three or four years older than she was. She was accustomed to being the center of boys' attention—and to dealing with that.

There was a boy my age, a junior, whose name also was Archie. My brother Archie, and Elsie, too, had graduated and gone to the US to college, while I was now on the top rung of the ladder, a senior. Archie proved to be my intense rival for Edna. He was rather handsome, which I was not; although he was not a good student, which I was. Edna played us off against each other, keeping both of us on her string. I was alternately elated and plunged in gloom. She would let me feel that she really enjoyed being with me, then would be talking and laughing with Archie, leaving me on the outside.

As the year ended, though, I felt that Edna was closer to me. I went off to college, taking her picture with me, an enlargement that I framed and kept on the wall of my room for a year, although I didn't hear anything more from her. Korea was far away, certainly in terms of correspondence. With my new life, a nostalgic idealization was enough—until that, too, began to fade.

With Bea, in time, there was a sort of revival. We made contact again, through another high-school friend. I was now engrossed in English studies at Princeton and was experimenting seriously with writing poetry. In one brief message, Bea wrote that she believed in me. That gave me a lift, and the theme of a lyric poem. Later, in my senior year, I made Bea an impulsive, quixotic proposal of marriage.

There was a Christian summer-conference center outside of Asheville, North Carolina, that my siblings and I had contact with and where we spent most of the summer of 1938. The center, called Ben Lippen, had a large, reconstructed building on a hilltop, and there was talk that summer about putting it to use during the school year by establishing an academy for boys. I naively thought that I could make a strong bid to be named principal or headmaster of the school.

It was my senior year at Princeton. Having a strong academic record, I wanted to try for a Rhodes Scholarship. Because my dad's three brothers and his sister all lived in Nebraska, he considered that his home state. As I had no home elsewhere in the United States, I was going to make my application from Nebraska, traveling out there during my winter vacation for an interview.

The trip to Nebraska by Greyhound bus would take me through Wooster, Ohio, and I knew that Bea was a student at Wooster College and living with her family there that year. What more natural than to arrange a stopover and a date with her?

We borrowed the family car and went for a drive. It was dream-like to be seeing Bea again and talking with her. I told her about Ben Lippen and the plans for the boys' school, and I proposed to her. We could begin a life together, serving in the new school. Would she do that?

It was quixotic, a completely imaginative proposal. Bea had her feet on the ground, much better than I. Her answer wasn't brusque, but it was clear enough; no. She knew me, even though we had been going our separate ways since graduating from PYFS. She told me how she had stayed in China for a year after graduation, and how she formed a close relationship with an American sailor in that place and time. These things are real, as she pointed out, but they pass.

We drove back to her house and, later that night, I was again on my way to Nebraska. As a footnote, my bid for a Rhodes was also unsuccessful.

*****

Let me turn back to PYFS and to a different memory from that time. We had a Boy Scout troop there. Its organizing scoutmaster, Mr. Shaw, was a strong figure, a missionary stationed in Pyongyang who had been in France in World War I—in the mud, gore, and gas attacks of the trenches. He wouldn't talk much about it, although he did collaborate, one year, as adviser for an original school play that had some dramatic, poignant war scenes. I don't know what rank he held in the Army—he had left that behind—but he was an excellent scoutmaster, using his free time and a blend of genial kindness and strict discipline to train us.

I was in eighth grade, as I remember it, when I started out as a Tenderfoot. Here was a ladder to be climbed. I worked my way up, passing each test, learning what needed to be learned, to arrive at First Class rank. Mr. Shaw made sure that the induction ceremony for First Class, held in the living room of his home, was solemn. A board held twelve candles, which the candidate was to light, one by one, as he recited the twelve Scout Laws.

This was a supreme moment for me, and I was approaching the final law. Then, suddenly, the room went dark. When I could see again, I was on a couch, looking at the ceiling and at Scoutmaster Shaw. He had seen the instant when I had started to faint. The room was warm; I had skipped dinner to be ready on time; and I was looking down at all those lighted candles. He moved so quickly that he caught me, before I would have gone, face down, on top of them.

Mr. Shaw did not continue with the scout troop, but Mr. Chandler, a teacher in our school, took it up. As we Scouts moved up in high school and there were other interests, many of the older boys dropped out. My brother, Archie, was getting more into sports and such. In his same grade, though, was Dave, who kept on with Scouting. Dave set his sights on being the first in our troop to reach the rank of Eagle Scout, and I wanted to follow him. Eagle meant earning twenty-one merit badges, of which, as I recall, Camping was one that was required.

Although I lived in the dorm with few resources, fortunately for me Dave's family was there in Pyongyang, and quite close by. His dad had found a good location for camping on the level ground beyond the Pothong River. Dave and I hiked out there. He had a pup tent that we set up. I think we even made a campfire, before we pushed ourselves into the pup tent for the night.

It was fascinating and a bit scary to be out there in dark solitude, just the two of us. We could hear an occasional sound from the village across the fields—a child's crying, some thumping sounds and a dog barking. Then it was quiet.

After a bit, abruptly, we sensed something moving quite close by. I clutched the tent flap, holding it tightly closed. The sound came close, and for a long moment there was a snuffling right at the edge of our tent. More sniffing, moving around to the other side, and then it went away.

"One of those village curs," Dave said. "They're always hungry. Good I didn't have any food out there in my back pack."

"Yeah," I answered, glad to have the assurance and to have silence again.

Dave achieved Eagle Scout rank that spring, before he graduated and left for college. I finished it in the fall. The Eagle Scout badge was like a medal, with the eagle suspended from a ribbon. A Scout could go on, after gaining the twenty-one merit badges for Eagle, and earn five more for a Bronze Palm, to pin on the Eagle ribbon. I did that—to enjoy the satisfaction of accomplishing something more and, I admit, to surpass Dave's mark.

Far back along the way since then, I lost that trophy. With so many moves and so many homes through the years, a number of valuables disappeared—among them, my Phi Beta Kappa key and the Eagle Scout badge.

5

Fear and Love of the Sea

SORAI BEACH—A BEAUTIFULLY SITUATED summer resort on the northwestern coast of Korea—how pleasant to evoke its past! Its beach and promontory lie above the Demilitarized Zone, in today's North Korea, so I know nothing of the present condition of the resort. No matter. I evoke it for its formative share in the fear and love relationship with the sea which I began to form there—an indelible part of my psyche.

I was not fortunate, as a child, to take naturally to water. At Sorai there were many children, including older ones who swam boisterously. Elsie and Archie were not at that point, but were on their way. Mother and we three children spent six or eight weeks at Sorai every summer, and Dad would take off two weeks at the hospital in Taegu to join us.

I've mentioned our cottage—a wondrous structure. Each family that purchased a lot at Sorai Beach would design and arrange for the construction of whatever sort of cottage they thought appropriate and within their means. Dad, quite typically, found a unique solution. He located a modest-sized, upper-class Korean pavilion not very far away that could be purchased and dismantled. He hired carpenters to remove the roof, tile by heavy clay tile, and disassemble the structure of the building, after the more-provisional clay or heavy paper partitions had been removed.

The main structure consisted of natural, round beams, cut at lengths to form eight-foot squares and then ingeniously notched to fit securely together. All of these parts, including the entire, gracefully curved roof, could be loaded on ox-carts and transported to our lot at the beach, where Dad had them re-assembled. It was then relatively easy for the carpenters to install a foreign-style wood floor plus walls and partitions, including large, hinged shutters that could be lifted and propped open in fair weather to allow a delightful breeze to blow through. Small windows on the shutters enabled them to be battened down securely when one of the occasional, driving rain-squalls of that region came up.

The cottage lot dropped away on one side, down a steep bank that was almost a cliff, perhaps some fifty feet, to a narrow band of rocks and stony beach, washed by the sea. The view, across some eight miles of bay to a low range of hills, was ever-changing in the changing light of sea and sky.

I did learn to swim, although never with any mastery. The Sorai Beach Association, made up of summer residents, established three levels of water skills, with simple tests by which one might qualify. The test for the third level was to swim, without a rest stop and without aid, from the swimming beach out around "the Point" (the main promontory) and down the length of the bluff where cottages were built, to the entrance of the fishing harbor—a distance of one-and-a-quarter miles. I managed this, in around ninth grade, and felt satisfied.

Meanwhile, there were the sailboats. Various residents contrived to build, or to have built, small, open ones. Archie, as one would expect, hung around the boathouse at the beach, where these were kept, and got chances to go out in some and to learn the elements of handling them. Elsie and I picked up his enthusiasm; so that when the children of one boating family went off to college and their boat was up for sale, we three put together gift money from relatives in the United States and bought the boat.

It was about twelve feet long, open and flat bottomed, but with good lines and a retractable centerboard to hold it on course. There was a mast near the bow, with a single, gaff-rigged sail. This had been one of the first sailboats at Sorai, and its appropriate name was *Veteran*. By the time we bought it, the community had seven or eight sailboats, enough to form a Sorai Beach Yacht Club and to organize a series of races in open water, well away from the promontory, but near enough for spectators with binoculars to watch.

We three entered our *Veteran* in the competition. The first year we lost to a competitor—a family that had just one son; but he was helped by an adult family friend who was an experienced sailor. In the second season, however, the competition was more even. Each racing day we three Fletchers would trudge the quarter-mile from our cottage to the swimming beach, carrying our sailing gear. Neighbors along the way would call out their encouragement and good wishes.

There was one tense incident. It involved the Underwoods, a prominent family in the community. The family's late grandfather had pioneered Presbyterian church work in Korea and had the vision to purchase the tract of land on which the Sorai Beach resort was built. Now, in this series of "yacht races," one of his grandsons and another boy were competing in the Underwoods' sailing canoe.

On one of the race days, there was an unusually stiff breeze—stiff enough to build up a frothing, choppy sea. We three were managing *Veteran* as well as we could, leaning out on the windward side and even letting our sail spill some wind. The sailing canoe was ahead of us, at times almost disappearing in the troughs between wave crests. Then, abruptly, as we looked for it again, it was gone. What we could make out was a curve of one side of the hull and the two heads of its crew bobbing beside it.

The Underwoods also had a cabin-cruiser sailboat with an outboard motor, which was functioning as the official boat for the race. It spotted the overturned canoe, came quickly to its aid, and in a short time had it righted, bailed out, and back in the race. Those details we found out later. What we knew at the time was that, after we rounded the final buoy and were on the homeward leg, the sailing canoe, running before the wind, which had definitely lightened, came up and passed us, to win the race.

That gave the officers of the Sorai Beach Yacht Club, adults who were in charge of racing rules, a head-scratching problem. Should the canoe be disqualified? It had won the race, but certainly received crucial help in order to do so. Without that help, could its two-boy crew have been able to get it righted and bailed out? The judges declared that they could have done that.

The solution adopted by the officials, desiring fervently to be fair and impartial, was to ask for and secure a calculation of the time it might have taken for the boys to get their canoe upright and afloat, to get themselves aboard, and to resume the race on their own, with no outside help—disregarding that in the windy, choppy sea such a feat would have been virtually impossible. Then, this time, so calculated, was added to the canoe's time for the race; which moved it back and gave our *Veteran* first place. It was a seemingly fair and reasonable resolution, but rankled them—the more so because, under Archie as captain and Elsie and me as crew, our *Veteran* went on to win the Sorai Yacht Club racing trophy that summer.

I remember a couple of other Sorai scenes that contributed to, or confirmed, my fear and love syndrome about the sea. One occurred on an evening when a storm was rolling in. Sorai had a normal tide of four or five feet, and sailboats were kept at the wide, gently-sloping swimming beach. The full arc of that beach of fine, white sand swept for three miles from the promontory on which the cottages were built. As the boats were kept anchored in shallow water, where we could wade out to them, the yacht club employed a man to care for them, lifting their anchors, and towing them in or out a couple of times a day, according to the tide.

On the evening I am remembering, when it was almost dark, there came a pounding on our door. It was a fellow boat owner, telling us that the surf was rising, and the boat-tender had to have help. All the boats must be hauled up beyond reach of the surf or they would pound on the sand. Dad was in Taegu, but Archie and I responded. We put on what seemed to be the best gear against the wind and a rain that was beginning to fall and hurried to the beach by what light was left, among roiling clouds.

At the beach several men and older boys were already at work with the boat-tender. The boathouse was built at the top of a gravel bank, and some of the craft had already been dragged up the bank, beyond the water's reach. It was an angry surf, as menacing as I had ever seen at Sorai, as the breakers frothed in through gathering darkness.

Then we saw the most urgent need. One of the newer boats had gotten away and been thrown up to where there were flat, but hard-edged, rocks. With each wave the boat was lifting and falling on rock. It wouldn't take long for it to be battered to pieces. Archie and I had put on our water shoes—old sneakers that served the purpose. He clambered onto the rock, along with two others, while all of us got whatever grip we could, and, just as a big wave lifted the boat, we hauled it free to safety.

That was a frightening surf. Sailors who go out in small boats know how dangerous surf is wherever it is breaking on rocks. I still feel a twinge, as I picture that boat in the almost-dark, lifting and falling on the rock.

On a very different, essentially tranquil day, we had hoisted our sail to a light breeze and pulled away, a few hundred yards from our home berth, when the breeze died. There were some clouds, and after a while we could make out the wispy front of a rain shower advancing slowly. The water around us was still, having subsided into a flat calm, and our sail hung slack.

Then there were drops—a few at first, then more—large drops falling around us. As each one struck the smooth surface of the water, a matching drop seemed to leap up to answer it, spreading a soft mist close to the quiet sea. Water wet our faces and soon began to sluice down the slack, useless sail. I knew I didn't care. It was, all of it, too beautiful, too transcendently serene. This was sea I could love, not fear.

6

Rolling for Eight Days and Nights

HIGH SCHOOL YEARS WERE approaching an end. In 1934 Elsie and Archie graduated. They had part of the summer at Sorai Beach, and Dad was there for his two weeks. Then they returned to Taegu with our parents, to get ready to leave for the United States and college—Elsie to Wilson College in Chambersburg, Pennsylvania, and Archie to Princeton. I was left at Sorai, with an agreement to invite a couple of high school boys to move in and share our cottage with me—a remarkable expression of trust on the part of Mother and Dad.

There were some boisterous times in the cottage in those "bachelor-club" days that we shared. One evening someone started a water fight, and soon we were splashing each other. A loud remonstrance stopped us. The patient cook whom Mother had left in charge of keeping us fed had her quarters downstairs in the half-basement, where the kitchen and laundry were also located. She came bursting up the stairs, declaring vigorously that water was dripping through the floor above her.

I was ashamed—because of the trouble we were causing her and also because I wanted to go along with my friends and to be part of the fun. I had let this foolishness go on and had an active share in it, forgetting my responsibility. A twist of that shame, too, still lingers.

After these days in the cottage, there was another unusual, maturing adventure that my parents agreed to, before the summer ended. One of our teachers at PYFS wanted to see something of the beautiful, much-noted Diamond Mountains on the eastern side of the Korean Peninsula. He offered to escort three other boys and me on a tour—a rare chance before we, too, would have to leave for college.

I have a few strong impressions from that four-day outing. On the first day we climbed one of the nearer, lesser peaks, eating our lunch and spending a while at the top. We were coming back down, pausing in a clearing by a pleasant pool, when one of my friends realized that he had left his camera up at the peak. It was his dad's camera, entrusted to him with many instructions. He had to recover it.

Our teacher escort recognized that there was nothing to do but to go back up the mountain with the camera boy. The other two members of the group said they would go back to the small inn where we were lodging, but I chose not to. The cool, shady setting of the pool was inviting. If that was all right, I would just wait there until the climbers came back down with the camera.

It is my nature that I have never minded being alone, as long as I'm not in confinement, and not for a very long time. This day, I sat on a bank. I watched the water, still except for a sleepy rivulet entering at one side, with apparently another across from it, departing. Occasionally, I thought I caught a glimpse of small fish beneath the surface, although they may have been the legs of swimming frogs. Above the water, some insects hovered in the warm air. I stood up and wandered along the pool's edge, my mind tranquilly occupied with this and that.

Sunlight in the glen seemed definitely to be taking on a yellow tinge when, finally, I heard the climbers returning. We were glad to get back to the Japanese inn, where our hostess had for us a supper of clear soup and steaming bowls of rice, accompanied by squares of dried seaweed and tasty condiments.

The next day we were to hike over a pass and descend to a town fronting on the Sea of Japan. A hardy mountaineer piled our suitcases on one of the conventional, ingeniously designed Korean racks adapted to his back with shoulder straps. Then he set off at a brisk pace, challenging our adolescent legs to keep up. Through long hours, walking behind him as we ascended by a steep path, I had in the forefront of my field of vision the bulging muscles of his calves maintaining an even rhythm. The next morning, our unaccustomed muscles were so stiff and sore we could hardly move. We watched with envy as some townsmen were emerging from a public bath, seeming to steam with jovial relaxation.

Later in the day, with groans, we got to the station and a train-ride to Seoul, from which I made it to Taegu and Mother and Dad. Elsie and Archie were gone, crossing the Pacific to college. Of us three, I was now alone at home; my turn to leave would come.

Of my senior year in high school, I've made some mention already, regarding affairs of the heart. It was a stimulating time—a time of adolescent ups and downs. After my other five years in boarding school in PYFS, this final one offered the exhilaration of being "on top," with no older students to look up to.

Our class decided to design blazers and have them made, at modest cost, by a downtown tailor. My share in the project was to come up with a class emblem for the front pocket. I drew on my love for Sorai Beach and sketched a stylized, double-sailed fishing junk, with PYFS spelled out on one tall sail and '35 on the other. Our class colors were orange and blue; so, the jackets were blue, and the junk had orange sails with dark blue lettering.

There were other proud moments in that senior year—as many of you have experienced in yours—but the year soon slipped by. My departure was coming up quickly. One missionary, a dentist whose family would be going on furlough, had discovered that by getting together enough travelers to form a group, all could ride the Trans-Siberian Railway to Europe for a surprisingly low figure. A number of us graduates joined in.

On the train I shared a compartment with three other boys. Our group chose "hard" rather than "soft" accommodations in a sleeping car, because our travel host had learned that the "soft" berths were likely to be "inhabited" and he didn't fancy having to deal with lice. One drawback was that I must pack for a new, college life in the US. Making the journey as we would be doing it, there was no way to check luggage—even a small trunk or foot-locker. Whatever I took must be in two large suitcases that I could hand-carry, and they did prove to be large. I nicknamed them Samson and Hercules, as I later hauled them on and off conveyances.

Boarding the train at Manchuli, on the Manchurian border with Siberia, we would ride it for six thousand miles, to Warsaw in Poland. That was like getting on in New York City, riding to San Francisco, then turning around and riding back to New York. We would be on the train for eight days and nights, rolling most of that time. Yet the cost of a ticket, at our group rate, was only sixty dollars ($60 US), coming out to about a hundred miles for a dollar.

Rolling for Eight Days and Nights

This was to be a grand adventure. After the excitement of graduation at PYFS, I was at home again, with only some short days to finish preparations for departure. I would be leaving Taegu, leaving behind Korea and my childhood and early adolescent years. I would be leaving Mother and Dad, whom I wouldn't see for two more years, until their furlough brought them to the United States. But I was sixteen. Nostalgic reflections were brushed aside by eager anticipation.

That was so, even when the moment came that we stood together on the Taegu station platform and my train whistled its departure. It was warmly reassuring, though, to have Mother's embrace, her moist-eyed, loving smile. Then Dad took my hand in his. He had never done that. It seemed that in giving me his hand, he was meeting me on his level—man to man. I climbed the steps to the sleeping-car, waving as the train began to move. As I left him and Mother on the platform, I took with me that powerful gesture of trust and confidence.

*****

On the way north, other members of our Trans-Siberia group got on, all buzzing with anticipation. When we arrived in Manchuli, there was our train, bright and clean, every brass fitting polished and gleaming. The locomotive was already beginning to huff, but we had some time, so we went to see something of Manchuli. This was 1935. It was a frontier town: an unpaved main street, muddy from recent rain, a few shops with fronts open to the early-summer air, then houses clustering together as the street became a road running out across grasslands toward the horizon.

One member of our group, who came from China and knew some Mandarin, was bargaining for some sweet cakes at a shop when our distant locomotive let loose a blast. For economy and perhaps health reasons, we were not going to use the train's dining car. Instead, each of us had with him a quantity of canned goods and other food for the week-long train ride. That day, our bargaining was cut short by the locomotive's hoot. We hurried back and clambered aboard.

We rode for many miles across wide steppes with wide horizons. Then we saw low hills, becoming mountains, densely forested. Signs of human habitation were few and stops at small stations infrequent. Also, as far north as we were, the days were long and the nights short, darkening slowly through a protracted dusk, then soon beginning to lighten into dawn.

In school at PYFS, many of us had paired off, as was natural. Now we were separated. I had left Edna, but in our group was Jean, without her boyfriend. One long evening I was standing with Jean at a window of the corridor that ran down one side of the car. The hour was late and the car quiet, as we talked in a leisurely way. It was quite dark, with forest all around. Our locomotive had labored up a long grade, topped it, and now was picking up speed. Where Jean and I stood, we were on the inside of a curve.

Suddenly there was a screech, and a violent pounding began right below, as the car started to rock. We could feel the brakes being thrown on; the pounding slowed, although the rocking became more pronounced. It all happened quite quickly. Everything stopped: no movement; silence. Then voices, as a couple of train operators with lanterns ran along the tracks, calling to each other.

Gradually we learned what had happened. Repeated rains had softened the railroad ties. As our car rounded that curve, the centrifugal force of its weight pushed the outside rail hard enough against the spikes in the ties that the rails spread apart, letting the car's inside wheels, which were right beneath Jean and me, drop off their rail and go pounding up and down on the ties. That was what made the screeching and made the car rock alarmingly. Fortunately, we were not moving fast, and the brakes were applied quickly.

We were in the Soviet Union. The mishap to its vaunted international train was played down to the passengers. In a surprisingly short time, that night, heavy railroad jacks were brought up. All passengers who were awake were told to stay in their compartments while the entire side of our car was lifted, the outside rail eased back in place and secured, and the car set back on the track. It started, cautiously, to roll again.

In Moscow there was a three-hour layover. The official Russian travel agency escorted all through-passengers to a hotel where refreshments and rest were provided. We four boys had heard that US dollars, which were exchanged for us at the government's official rate, could be traded on the street for many more rubles, as the people were eager to get dollars. We slipped surreptitiously out of the hotel to try that out, just to assert our freedom; but when we tried slyly to offer crisp dollar bills to pedestrians who appeared to be good prospects, all we got were blank stares or, even, in a couple of cases, some angry words. So much for that.

In Warsaw we left our train, once so polished and shining, now streaked and bedraggled. Our Korea travel group broke up, but we four boys stayed together to see what we could of Europe while our money held out. From Warsaw, we went to Berlin. Germany was expensive, however, and not appealing. This was 1935, and the Nazis' brown shirts and swastikas were already evident, although the gigantic shadows of what was to come were, as yet, indistinct to us.

I did, however, have a chance to carry out a personal plan. On our family furlough six years earlier, our grandparents on Mother's side had observed their fiftieth wedding anniversary by giving Elsie, Archie and me, each of us, five ten-dollar gold coins. I had kept mine and, before this trip, turned them into traveler's cheques, with which I now purchased a Rolleicord, my first fine camera.

From Germany, we went to the Netherlands, and there heard about taking a boat from Rotterdam up the scenic River Rhine. Cabin accommodations would cost more than we wanted to spend; but it was summer, so we could buy cheap tickets and sleep on deck. In effect, the nights proved chillier than we anticipated. I had two sweaters; so, at night, after cabin passengers had retired, I wore one normally and the other upside down, to keep my legs warm. Also, we found a steel plate that covered a vent from the engine room. It was a hard surface to sleep on; but it was warm.

By day, we marveled at the castles that we passed on the river banks and heights above, and I kept photographing them, thinking that each one might be the last. For daily fare we had bought in Rotterdam a supply of bread, tomatoes and cheeses. These served us well, with some occasional small purchases. Young people, when on an adventure, will adapt resourcefully to almost any conditions.

We left the boat at Mannheim and proceeded into Switzerland but found that country too expensive and bought tickets to Paris. In good spirits, we were approaching the border when the French inspector, coming through the train, asked to see our passports. Suddenly, my heart sank. There had been a time problem with securing a French tourist visa before I left Korea, so I had strict instructions to negotiate that at a French consulate in Warsaw or in Germany. Of course, I forgot about it. Now the inspector looked at my passport, listened to my fumbling explanation in my high school French, and said curtly, as we were stopped at a station just short of the French border,

"*Descendez avec vos bagages.*"

That command I could understand all too well. There was nothing to do, now, but to lower Samson and Hercules to the platform, hurriedly agreeing to meet my companions the next morning, at the US Consulate in Paris. The Swiss official I spoke with at the railroad station office was more helpful. He instructed me to take the next train, a local, and get off at the first station, which would be in France. There I should go to the border official and request, with probable success, a French tourist visa. They were accustomed to dealing with tourists who found themselves in such predicaments.

I did as instructed, got to the small station, and received, stamped in my passport, that all-important visa. It would be a while, I learned, before the next train for Paris came along. I left my suitcases where I could keep an eye on them and walked the narrow platform beside the tracks. Dusk was falling. Behind the ridge of a dark hill to the west, a reddish glow was giving way to gray. Out on that platform there was no voice, no sound. I was alone.

My spirit was buoyed, however, by the consideration I had been shown. My passport held that official stamp. My friends had gone on ahead; they might be nearing Paris; but they would meet me. In the gathering dark and the unfamiliar place, the solitary feeling of it might have been unnerving. I felt a strong impression of it, as I do again now in recreating it; but I felt calm. I could be content to wait. Eventually, there was the noise and brightness of the locomotive headlight on the track.

The train was a local. It was early morning when we reached Paris. I found a locker where I could leave my luggage, and at a newsstand I bought a map of the city. When I located the US Consulate on the map, it looked to be far from the railroad station. No matter; there was plenty of time to walk it, and I definitely would not use my hoarded money on a cab. I started out. There was a fascination in navigating by the map, reading names of the principal streets and seeing those names posted. I had gone some distance and was threading a maze of smaller streets when I saw a café that was open.

I asked for bread and coffee. The genial host brought out a warm loaf that looked to be a yard long and asked me to mark out the length I wanted. How delightful, doubly so when breaking and munching that oven-fresh, real French bread.

Another pleasure awaited in store. Leaving the café, I turned a corner onto a street that ran to the River Seine. When I looked the far length of it, there in the distant morning light was Notre Dame! I knew it from pictures, of course, beginning with a pored-over plate in a set of *Art and Architecture* photographs that we received in Taegu from the Calvert School; but this was the real thing. That first glimpse had a romantic magic that closer views that same day, and on visits in much later years, could never quite recapture.

My three travel companions did show up at the US Consulate, sleepy-eyed and rather tardy. We did some sightseeing. Then two of our group left to board a ship for New York. The third, Clyde, and I crossed the Channel for London and the final part of our college-bound journey to the United States—the "homeland," as I had heard it called in my childhood, although it wasn't home to me.

One of my cousins had married an Englishman, and they lived in a London suburb. Dad had arranged with them by mail for Clid and me to visit. (We shortened the long vowel in Clyde's name to make it easier to say.) It was wonderful for us that my cousin Joan had planned a series of sight-seeing days, taking care of transportation, tickets, and every detail. Some highlights were the British Museum, the outdoor Whipsnade Zoo, and, by a lucky timing coincidence, tennis at Wimbledon, where my recollection is that we saw Don Budge, then one of the world's best.

We saw the tennis up close. Joan had secured standing-room and sent us there early, to get right next to a low fence. The sun beat down on us directly there, and I had, predictably, forgotten to take a hat. At one point I actually fainted, crouched down against the wire netting; but Clid helped me and it passed over. There was no way to get out through the crowd without causing a lot of commotion.

When our London days were done, we boarded ship in Southampton for New York. Clid and I mentioned to some fellow passengers that we were both Princeton students. One day when we were wearing our senior-class jackets from PYFS, one of those passengers eyed us up and down and said, "So, you boys are from Princeton?" I don't recall what lame rejoinder we had as an answer to that.

As our ship came up New York Harbor, I thrilled, as have so many millions, to see the Statue of Liberty. We docked and Clid went his way, but no-one was there to meet me. I learned afterward that in fact my grandfather Dada was there, but through some confusion he couldn't make connections. I wasn't upset. This was New York. I was actually there!

I knew that Elsie and Archie were working that summer at a conference center called Silver Bay, located on Lake George in upper New York State. The plan was that on arrival I should take a bus to the town of Lake George, at the southern end, and then a boat that cruised the lake, buying my passage to Silver Bay. The first thing, then, was to go to the New York bus station, which I did, finding that the upstate bus would not leave until early evening. Fine; that would mean quite a few hours there in the city.

As I'd done in Paris, I left my suitcases in a locker and started out—only that this time I had no map and no specific destination. A destination of sorts was the Empire State Building, which I knew only from pictures. As I walked the Manhattan streets, I first glimpsed the Chrysler Building, which I also recognized. When I finally came to the Empire State, the fee to ride an elevator to the top seemed steep to me, and I wasn't sure that I wanted to go up there, anyway. I contented myself with gazing from the sidewalk.

There was more time to kill. I came on a theater advertising a continually running film titled *Vampire of the South Seas*. In Pyongyang, American movies seldom made it to a downtown theater, and it was very seldom that our school organized an escorted outing to see one. So, I bought a ticket and went in. The mediocre film had just begun. I saw it to the end, and my watch showed that there were still several hours until the bus left. I watched the film again, all the way through, emerging groggily into late afternoon to buy a cheap meal, then wait some more at the station until I could board my bus.

All night we rolled northward, as I dozed off and on. The town of Lake George, in the morning, was bright and lively. The boat was there, but there was more waiting until the strong baritone of its horn announced departure. That voyage was fascinating—the people getting on and off along the way, their bright colors reflected on ripples in the clear lake water.

It was early afternoon when the voice from the speaker announced, "Silver Bay." As we drew closer, there was Archie, waving to me from the dock. Elsie, he explained, was working. She was a waitress, and it was approaching tea time. His job was driver of the all-purpose truck, and no task was pending.

How fulfilling it was to be together again—and how different. We'd had a year, moving on distinct trajectories, he and Elsie in their new college worlds; I in the old scene, but an experimentally dominant role. I was glad, though, to again be part of "us three." That was reassuring.

The Silver Bay Association, which operated a large, central hotel and auditorium, with outbuildings and grounds, all beautifully situated on scenic Lake George, employed many college students for its summer program. The pay was meager, but the hours for most were short; and it was a huge benefit to have room and board all summer in a magnificent setting, with congenial companion employees from many schools. For the remaining weeks of that summer I worked with Archie on the truck, happy to belong to "the emps of Silver Bay," as one of our employee songs had it.

7

"In Praise of Old Nassau"

Leaving Silver Bay, we three had a week or so in Ridley Park, Pennsylvania: 414 Swarthmore Avenue. That was our grandparents' address, and it became our home address in the United States over our college years and for some time beyond. The house was situated on a tree-shaded street in a comfortable suburb of Philadelphia where Robert Rodgers, Mother's father, established his family when they moved out of the city.

The family was there when their daughter Jessie first went to Korea, and still there when Elsie and Archie came back to college. We three had many vacations, or parts of our vacations, sleeping in two rooms on the third floor, up under the roof, and enjoying family times at the dinner table and in the living room. From the Rodgers' house, in this September 1935, Elsie went to Wilson College for her second year, and Archie and I to Princeton, where he had broken ground for me in his solitary, sometimes difficult freshman year.

> Tune every heart and every voice.
> Bid every care withdraw.
> Let all with one accord rejoice
> In praise of Old Nassau.

So, go the opening lines of Princeton's traditional song—the one that includes, at the refrain, a solemn, right-hand wave, from over the heart to a wide-open gesture. I learned the song eagerly, proud that I could share it as my own.

"In Praise of Old Nassau"

Princeton University—for me this was, in truth, a "brave new world"! Archie and I had a suite, more modest than the word implies: a bedroom for each and a small front living room to share—on the second floor of old Reunion Hall, since torn down. We both had jobs waiting table in the Underclass Commons in Holder Hall, and, over the course of the years, worked at some other on-campus jobs. Generally, the pay was quite good. Most of the friends we made were also working, in various student agencies that offered services on campus. We used to joke that half of us students lived off the other half.

The university to me was a marvelously fresh, intriguing, revolutionizing place. In English 101—Freshman English—there were lectures such as I had not even faintly experienced before. The large lecture hall, its sloping floor filled to the back with tier on tier of students, each with a note pad on the wide writing-arm of his seat, both awed and thrilled me. I had never heard such teaching, such discourse delivered with superb poise and finesse. One or two of the lecturers possessed a command of the literary world they were presenting to us that was so complete my imagination was carried away. Sometimes, when the lecturer ended with an adroit flourish and the distant bell on Nassau Hall was ringing, I could hardly get my feet on the floor again and find my way to the lecture hall door.

That was the case when J. Duncan Spaeth, master Shakespeare scholar, was lecturing to more advanced students. Hearing that he was about to leave Princeton, I managed to attend one of his final lectures. What a rarefied atmosphere I, a freshman, was given to breathe. I can also remember, on more than one evening, standing under the arch of Blair Hall, looking down the long flight of stone steps to the irregular quadrangle of the lower campus, seeing dormitory windows alight, hearing voices and music, and exulting in the feeling, without formulating it, that all this was now mine. After the sheltered restriction of my childhood and my earlier education at PYFS, this was a wonderful vista.

At that time, on a more mundane level, all entering students had to pass certain physical tests. There was water safety—the ability to swim. I had no trouble with that. What was harder was a pair of tests in the gym. One had to hoist himself (no women at Princeton then) a short distance up a free-hanging rope, using hands and feet, within a prescribed number of seconds. And hanging by a grip on the top of a smooth wood partition, he was required to get himself up and over it—again, within the seconds prescribed. I wasn't able to pass either of these climbing tests.

Those who failed were enrolled in a required body-building class. There was one way to get out, which was to be listed in a qualifying sport. I found that the 150–pound crew was one of these. I was too light for regular crew, so that had an immediate appeal.

That fall I discovered that the walk to the boathouse was a delight. It made a long, gradual descent through the last buildings, across some open, grassy slopes, to the lower edge of campus, where it bordered on Lake Carnegie. The lake, which bears the name of Scottish American financier Andrew Carnegie, is long, but not wide, affording an excellent waterway for rowing competitions. There are trees along the path leading down to it and many other trees on lakeside properties; and that autumn their colors seemed particularly brilliant. I exulted in their display.

We beginning rowers were assigned to practice boats of eight. They were somewhat heavier and sturdier than sleek shells that more advanced oarsmen rowed but had the same rolling seats; the oarlocks were mounted on frames that reached away from the boat, out over the water, to permit the rhythmic dip and thrust of the long oars. Since some of us were new to the sport, our coach, riding nearby in a launch, would stop us on the open water for a break, while he gave us pointers through a megaphone. During those intervals my mind easily wandered, drawn away by the beauty of the setting and my wonder at just being there. I recall one time when the coach singled me out.

"Hey, Number Four, pay attention; this is for you, too. Number Four!"

Number Three, behind me said in a loud whisper,

"Four, he means you."

Abashed, I turned my whole attention to the launch. A good thing for me about 150-pound crew, as also the regular crew, was that it went on through the winter. When it was getting too cold to be out on the lake, we were moved inside to a sunny annex to the gym, where there were rows of rolling seats, just like those in the shells, and oars with the same grips and movement, only that the oars were cut off at the oarlock and offered a resistance that could be adjusted.

My body-building effort continued, to my benefit. At the end of spring practice, for which we again took to the lake, I reported for a retake on those gymnastics tests, climbing the rope and getting over the wall. This time they didn't seem so formidable. I was glad that I could do them both, and within the allotted number of seconds.

"In Praise of Old Nassau"

A different aspect of university life for me, during my years there, was my religious orientation. I have thought about this a good deal, and with some regret; but that is how it was. My background and upbringing was in a strongly evangelical form of Christian faith. This I absorbed from childhood and, in adolescence, chose to hold to it.

Perhaps the choice was not so freely made. After leaving home, I maintained a close relationship with my sister and brother, both of whom followed this path unquestioningly. In addition, at Princeton there was the Princeton Evangelical Fellowship (PEF). That was a very small group of students of similar backgrounds and persuasion, shepherded by Donald Fullerton, a fervently evangelical layperson who lived in a nearby town. Archie had, quite naturally, affiliated himself with the PEF, and I followed suit. The group afforded some stability, but also some tension. Evangelicalism tends to stress a difference from "the world" that the believer should feel and practice. It is there in the New Testament, in letters of Paul and the Pastoral Epistles—natural and needed in the first and second centuries of the Christian movement. Believers then had to hold to their faith in Christ and strong contrast to the idolatrous and sometimes immoral practices of the pagan society around them. To what degree was a similar thrust appropriate in the society of Princeton University in the later 1930s?

I was by nature, and still am, not spontaneously outgoing and gregarious, and this sort of evangelicalism did not help. It tended to hold me back from freely participating in the social life of the university. In addition, a tenet of this interpretation of Christian faith is that the believer should constantly be ready to "witness" to her or his conviction. This is held to be, in a real sense, the reason for her/his being in the world—to confront worldly people and practices with the Gospel—tactfully, but very plainly and directly. That was also often on my mind in those undergraduate years—no doubt as a further inhibition. I have felt it still, particularly in reunion gatherings of one-time classmates. My friendships were few, and mostly superficial. As of the present, to be sure, very few classmates are still alive.

My junior year at Princeton was different. Mother and Dad were on furlough from Korea. They had extended their current term there by a year so that the furlough (in the States) would coincide with Elsie's and Archie's final college year and they could be present for my siblings' graduations. Once again, they had the use of one of the Payne Hall apartments on Princeton's Alexander Street, so that Archie and I were able to live "at home" for the academic year. We shared one of the two bedrooms of the apartment, across the street from Princeton Theological Seminary and just a block from one edge of the university campus. The side street on which our window opened was lined with maples that, in the autumn, turned a brilliant yellow, flooding our room with golden light.

In my studies I had turned a corner. As I entered college, I had thought that I would go on to study medicine. That was the direction Archie was taking; and further, during my last high school vacations in Taegu, when I was there alone, I had found it interesting and stimulating to spend time at the hospital, working in the lab. Dad's chief laboratory technician, Mr. Suh, had been in the United States and was fluent in English, and he possessed a congenial personality. I enjoyed learning from him. Hence, at Princeton I took chemistry and physics courses, as well as liberal arts, planning on medicine. But that direction had gradually been changing. Although Archie was majoring in chemistry, I chose English. What might that lead to? Given my background and upbringing, the Christian ministry was a possibility, although I had no distinct sense of a "call" to that career.

I remember one spring evening of that year. My parents had a visitor—was it Dr. McCune? I don't remember for sure, although McCune was a highly regarded missionary in Pyongyang, an educator whom I had known there. What I do recall well is that, at his suggestion, we went out to sit on the front steps of Payne Hall, enjoying the soft evening air. In the semi-darkness he talked with me about my plans. My grades were high, especially in my English subjects. I should set my mark high: why not toward being president or provost of a college or university—have a goal like that from the beginning and work toward it.

We were sitting directly across from the massive shadow of the Seminary's Stuart Hall, but McCune (if that's who he was) didn't talk about the ministry. He seemed to assume that I was pointed toward an academic career. I've often reflected, over the years, on that evening conversation. Had my parents suggested it to their guest? For me it was memorable, although not a deciding factor.

Archie was in line for Phi Beta Kappa that year, and I learned that I, too, would be inducted. At Princeton then, to make Phi Beta Kappa in junior year was to be part of a very small group. Our parents took both of us to buy tuxedoes for the formal induction dinner, which would be in the beautiful neo-Gothic dining hall of the Graduate College. Such an expenditure was unusual for our family.

"In Praise of Old Nassau"

After Elsie's and Archie's graduations, from Wilson College and Princeton, Mother and Dad left to return to Taegu. We three went to North Carolina, to Ben Lippen, the conservative Christian conference center I mentioned earlier. Women students could live there on the top floor of the main building and earn board and room as housekeepers or by waiting tables. For men, there was Lippen Lodge, a rustic structure a ways into the woods. Located along a ridge, the lodge had a fine view across rolling country toward the Blue Ridge mountains. The spartan accommodations included a kitchen where the males did our own cooking.

Evening gatherings, usually a part of conferences at the Center, were held in the Tabernacle, which was simply a roof on pillars with side walls that could be opened out in pleasant weather. There were inspirational speakers, all strongly in the evangelical tradition. And there might simultaneously be a magnificent sunset above the darkening western skyline.

Much of this was inspiring. There was one class in particular, a session in one of the conferences, that I enjoyed. It was taught by the Rev. Dr. H. Framer Smith, and the subject was Homiletics, the Art of Preaching. This course was ordinarily taught in a theological seminary. Dr. Smith was adapting it, because in the evangelical tradition, young Christians such as ourselves might engage in street preaching or similar public witnessing to our faith. As I look back on that summer, I see how my bent toward the ministry was being gradually affirmed.

Dr. Smith had his family with him at Ben Lippen—his wife, son Elwyn, and daughter Ethel. Elwyn was living at the lodge, and we struck up an immediate friendship. We had similar interests and were at a similar point in our studies and development. Elwyn had adventurous ideas. He came up with a plan that we two could spend two weeks canoeing on the Minnesota forest waterways. The Smith family was driving to New York City, where Dr. Smith had a medical appointment. I would go with them, and Elwyn and I would take it from there. Archie was a bit doubtful about this; but I felt confident.

The Minnesota canoe trip did not materialize. Dr. Smith's appointment turned out to be for an eye problem that led to surgery, and only after long delays. Elwyn and I stayed in various places while we waited to start our trip, even returning to Princeton to camp, provisionally, in the two-room dorm suite that I had for my coming senior year. As our plan dwindled away, so did the last of our summer.

8

Beer Jackets and Pine Logs

WITH SEPTEMBER, MY SENIOR year was now unfolding. I was on my own. Archie was beginning his medical studies in New York City, at Columbia University's College of Physicians and Surgeons. In the north entry of Princeton's massive, stone Dodd Hall, there were three of us, good friends lodged one above the other—Bill Stoll on the first floor, I on the second, and John Jansen on the third. John and I were both English majors and had been participants in the Princeton Evangelical Fellowship—although we were letting this latter slide. We would, from time to time, get together in the late evening in his suite or in mine, to relax from study and to chat about our courses or our interests and experiences relating to girls we were meeting.

For me that fall and winter, there was a young woman named Eloyce. Beaver College, in Philadelphia, was having a festive dance, and Huldah Blair, our companion when my siblings and I were children in Taegu, Korea, was now a student at Beaver. She arranged for a friend, Eloyce, to invite me for the weekend. After the dance, we drove to Eloyce's home, quite near, for chocolate cake she had made and some late-evening talk. The next morning, Sunday, her father hosted me in his Bible class for men, which they called the Iron Rose. I found the visit, and Eloyce, pleasant, as I later wrote to her.

Then came the winter break and my trip to Nebraska to try for a Rhodes Scholarship, which I mentioned in chapter 4. In Orchard, I stayed with my Uncle Gordon and Aunt Myra. She teased me when a package came with a large studio photo of Eloyce. Was this my girlfriend and was our relationship serious? No, I said, she was just a girl at Beaver College who invited me to their winter holiday dance. Aunt Myra smiled knowingly at that, and let it pass. On into early spring I exchanged a note or two with Eloyce, but was careful to keep the friendship casual, letting it die away. The photograph went into a drawer, and was, in time, discarded.

At Princeton I was reveling in the advanced English courses that I was taking, and particularly in the preceptorials. The university was proud of the system which combined lectures in a subject with small discussion groups, each to meet with a "preceptor." I was also finding pleasure and stimulation in poetry. From childhood, I had been fascinated by the music of language and had tried my hand at writing verse. Now I began to produce a lot more.

This is not the place for an anthology of poems. Let me simply recall that I wrote about Beatrice in chapter 4, how my school-days crush on her carried over into the quixotic proposal on my same trip to try for a Rhodes scholarship. She declined, but in the spring wrote a note in which she said that she believed in me, in what I might be able to accomplish. That prompted a lyric, which I never sent to her. I include it here to let it show my romanticism, with rather elaborate decoration. Its date is March 7, 1939:

> In the shade of my night-stilled heart,
> Sacred to memory
> I erect this shrine apart,
> Because you believe in me.
>
> Trees that are laden with Spring
> Whisper their fragrance here,
> And a flame-gold bird may sing
> In the youth of the year,
>
> And the breeze blow out and in
> The porticoes lingeringly;
> Unloveliness here be sin,
> Because you believe in me.
>
> When my spirit, walking near,
> Tired, in the cool of the day,
> Hears, or thinks to hear,
> Where the falling fountains play,
>
> Your voice, I know it sighs

> Where the censer steams; I see
> Your form and your shadowy eyes,
> Because you believe in me.

This was my senior spring. I eagerly followed the tradition of "beer jackets." Seniors purchased and wore white denim painters' jackets that bore, on the right rear shoulder, a symbolic design etched in black. Some creative classmates produced the design, which represented our Class of '39s distinctive achievements. Bill Stoll, John Jansen, and I, along with a few others, wore our beer jackets on an outing to New York City to see something of the 1939 World's Fair. I was deeply impressed by the almost-bare pavilion of Czechoslovakia, and the motto displayed on the World's Fair medal for the country: "Czechoslovakia shall be free again." Hitler's *Wehrmacht* was on the move and had taken over.

At our remote and tranquil distance, there was not yet much alarm. We saw by the newsreel in our local theater that image of Chamberlain descending from a plane at London's airport, umbrella in hand, to assure his country that his mission to Germany had been successful. There would be "peace in our time."

Ironic as that assurance proved to be, at Princeton our life was indeed peaceful. Savoring all the senior class traditions, I joined in the Step Sings. On a pleasant spring evening, members of the soon-to-graduate Class would assemble on the front steps of Nassau Hall to sing Princeton songs and a few other folk favorites, watching the dusk gather in the tall elm trees. Beer jackets were, naturally, the favored costume. I didn't drink beer—abstention from alcohol was part of my inherited tradition—but I was proud of my beer jacket.

By this relaxing time, we had behind us Princeton's redoubtable requirement—the senior thesis. Specifics would vary according to the departmental requirements for one's major. My thesis was perhaps more creative than scholarly. Several younger faculty members in liberal arts were in those days talking and writing about aesthetic theory, and, with my penchant for lyric poetry, I picked up on that. My thesis adviser, Prof. Murch, had taught an elective on Creative Writing, a course I had taken. Thus, my thesis came to be "On the Nature of Pure Lyric," an ambitious exploration of the lyric poem and how it comes to be composed.

The thesis had a firm due date, and like others, I was working late hours, pushing hard to get it finished. Coffee helped, but not enough. I wondered if tobacco might work and, for the first time in my life, bought and smoked a couple of packs of cigarettes.

It was later, after the pressure was off, that I went up to New York City for a weekend with Archie, sleeping on a cot in his narrow dorm room and learning about the life of a first-year medical student. From his window, at night, he had a beautiful view of the lights that festooned the graceful inverted arc of George Washington Bridge. In our talk, I told him about my experiment with smoking to try to keep working late. On his suggestion, we promised that if either of us turned to tobacco in the future, he would frankly tell the other. That's how Archie was, and I felt good about it.

Back in Princeton, at year's end a final hurdle was the Comprehensive Examination. The senior "Comp" in English spanned several hours and, under the terms of the university's honor code, it could be taken anywhere. I did mine on my Remington portable typewriter in my dorm suite, no doubt with something of a rhetorical flourish. Over the years, facility with language has been, for me, a mixed blessing, sometimes conveying more depth or knowledge than I have.

At that time, the ranking given each prospective graduate was posted, by academic department, in Nassau Hall some few days before commencement. I went, with bated anticipation, to scan the lists. There was my name, with *"summa cum laude"* following it! I felt staggered, both thrilled and humbled. I went down the list of fifty classmates in the English department. There were others with high honors, but no other *summa*. Scanning all the other departmental listings, I saw just five more *summa* designations—six of us in a class of around six hundred.

The next day, I think it was, I had a note asking me to go by the office of Dean Root, the Academic Dean, who was also a professor in the English Department. The dean received me with cordial formality; his manner was always impeccably correct. He informed me that, as the first-ranking graduate in English, I was eligible to receive a specific fellowship for a year of expense-free graduate study at the university. Dean Root knew of my intention to prepare for the ministry and noted that the PhD in English at Princeton was clearly oriented toward an academic career. He presumed that I would step aside, and the fellowship would go to the next-in-line graduate.

"I will gratefully accept the fellowship," I said. "I have the highest regard for our Department."

The Dean maintained his courteous composure, and my plan was set, at least for the one year. An ironic touch, and a tribute to the person who was Dean Robert K. Root, came some four years later. After pursuing both graduate study in English and completing the full course at the theological seminary, I reached the point of selecting an area in which to write my doctoral dissertation. Wanting to bring the two fields together, and reflecting my strong interest in lyric poetry, I looked to Isaac Watts, the pioneering eighteenth-century hymn writer. Dean Root was the English Department's Eighteenth-Century specialist, so I was assigned to him. Be it said, that he was unfailingly kind and helpful, always in his very correct way. With his guidance, I planned and successfully produced a full-length dissertation, "English Psalmody and Isaac Watts."

Here, again, was a new and different environment. To start with, I was lodged in Princeton's Graduate College, the beautiful Neo-Gothic structure set on a rise at the edge of the municipal golf course, a half-mile distant from the rest of the campus. The college is dominated impressively, and most artistically, by Cleveland Tower, with its masterful carillon.

The suite assigned to me was on the ground floor. My living room windows opened on a central quadrangle, while the bedroom windows looked across the sloping golf course to a pond, beyond which was the historic, elegant Princeton Inn (later to become Forbes College, an undergraduate residential facility). Dinners were served in the vaulted Procter Hall, where in spring the late sunlight illumined soaring stained-glass windows depicting themes of Arthurian legend. We students were expected to wear academic gowns to dinner; which I gladly did, although some fellow students observed the letter of the law by reducing the gown to a sleeveless black vest.

All of that was paid by my fellowship, and I breathed it in deeply. There was one evening when I stood in the quadrangle, outside my entry. The news had been reporting the Soviet invasion of Finland, and high in Cleveland Tower the carillon began to sound, ringing out poignantly the magnificent melody of Sibelius' "Finlandia." What a world to be part of!

There was something else that year, on a more modest scale, in which I had a hand. I knew that Ethel Smith, Elwyn's sister, was starting, in September, at Westminster Choir College, a music school on the northern edge of the town and decided that I should welcome her to Princeton. It was not like me to be diligent about social niceties; but this time I would do it. Westminster Choir College was short on dormitory space; its Freshman

House, that year, was a large home on Nassau Street, rented and adapted to house freshman girls. Ethel met me at the door, and immediately inside, in the front hallway, several girls were doing their ironing. Calling one of them over, Ethel said,

"This is one of my new friends, Martha Bradway. Her father is a Methodist pastor in Trenton."

As I stayed to chat a little while, I noticed Martha to be a lively, obviously bright teenager. It seems, as things turned out, that she noticed me rather more carefully.

At the First Presbyterian Church on the edge of the university campus, which Archie and I had attended from our early student days, there was a student youth group. With my evangelical leaning, I had found it liberal and unappealing. Now, with Ethel, Martha, and several others, including the daughter of the then-president of theological seminary, we formed a plan. The First Presbyterian youth group would be electing officers for its new academic year. We staged a coup and, voting as a bloc, put ourselves in.

This meant, of course, that we continued to see one another in youth-group meetings, as well as the usual Sunday evening open discussions. I recall, one dark fall night, offering to walk Elena, the seminary president's daughter, home after we officers had met. I didn't know until long afterward that Martha took much notice of that, wishing (in her own telling) that she was the one I was seeing home. I was happy, though, to be invited to Springdale, Dr. Mackay's residence, and to chat with Elena and her mother. I'm sure I stayed too long but did get a chance to speak with Dr. Mackay when he came out of his study to greet me. The Mackays had been missionaries in Peru, and he was known for his scholarly mastery of Spanish and Latin culture. When at length I left, he not only saw me to the door, but stood watching as I walked down the long driveway and waved when I finally turned the corner.

Throughout that graduate year, I was thus seeing Martha Bradway from time to time. My college friend John Jansen, now in his first year at the seminary, was also in our youth group. He and I made plans for a string quartet concert being offered in one of the large lecture halls in the university. I invited Ethel to be my date, and John invited Martha. Naive as I was, I had no inkling that Martha was paying more attention to me than to John when we got together at intermission and when we walked the girls back to their dorm.

*****

When spring came, bringing with it the end of my fellowship year, I knew I would be changing direction. I couldn't afford further graduate study in English on my own. In seminary, costs were much lower and there would be financial assistance—and the ministry was the career that I had come to feel distinctly to be my calling. Meanwhile, however, a new summer project was filling my foreground.

Elwyn Smith, now a graduate student at Harvard and always adventurous, had come to know a wooded ravine near Rumney, New Hampshire. He had bought a half-acre lot, accessible by a winding dirt road that followed the ravine's mountain creek. From the road, the lot sloped up quite steeply to the rounded top of a ridge. Elwyn's idea was to build a log cabin on the ridge. There must be people up the road, but from his ridge, no dwelling nor building lot was in sight.

I took up the idea and managed to get together a few hundred dollars, which made me a 50/50 owner of the lot. A windstorm had blown down a number of tall, straight pines, which made a natural beginning for the log-cabin project. We discovered that on some of the fallen trees, ants had been chewing the sweet layer under the bark; that made it easy to peel the trunks clean and ready them to be sawed into lengths for our cabin. It was hard, absorbing work; but we found it possible, for just the two of us, to pry and drag the cut logs up the slope, and notch them, ready to fit them together to form the walls of a modest cabin. There was the planning and building of a foundation, and later a fireplace lined with tempered brick and a sheet-metal flu that we secured in the village.

Our academic studies hadn't taught us to handle such tasks, so the challenges were part of the adventure. For one week, my sister Elsie came and camped with us on our lot, taking over the campfire cooking and improving our diet.

To do laundry, we had the lovely mountain stream right across the road, at the bottom of our lot. By happy chance it had formed a pool there among the boulders that was deep enough for swimming and even a shallow dive off a rock at one side.

Nights could be dark and a bit solitary, but people native to the area assured us that there were no bears nearby and no wolves to howl at the moon. Outside the tent flap at night one might, at most, hear some small, nocturnal creature scurry among the leaves.

Elwyn's family was in nearby Rumney for a week. His father, a minister and Bible teacher, was leading a study session at a summer conference held by two of the churches.

There was one near-accident in our construction while they were there. One day the Rev. Dr. Smith, who was short and a bit portly, came to help with clearing and trimming. We had our walls up nearly full height by this time, and Elwyn and I were working a final log into position, when it slipped and started to fall. Dr. Smith was working directly below. We both yelled—which was all we could do.

Elwyn's dad looked up and saw the teetering log. He wasn't spry enough to jump and run. He just turned, opened his arms, and somehow caught the log as it came at him. It seemed an astounding feat—totally improbable—but showed what the physical organism can do in an extreme situation. We were absolutely careful, after that, to be certain that no one was below where we were working.

Did we finish the cabin? We got it roofed over and made secure for the winter. That was my only summer at the cabin, but Elwyn later bought out my share. While at Harvard, he was near enough to get over and see the cabin made habitable; such that, after his marriage, and with some addition, it came to be his family's beloved vacation home, serving for many years. After Elwyn's wife died and he moved to Florida, it changed hands; but, to my knowledge, the Rumney cabin is still there and still in use.

9

Martha

LET ME GO BACK to late spring of 1940, as my fellowship year of graduate study in English was drawing to a close. I made a date with Martha for the spring concert of the Westminster Choir, the college's touring choir. It was a formal dress event for students, presented in Princeton's McCarter Theater.

On this evening I really noticed her—noticed to a point of fascination. Her long dress was a sheath of raspberry silk that set off her slim, rather boyish figure. We talked and laughed in a group of her fellow students at the concert intermission. She knew she was fascinating me—tossing the brown curls she had carefully set, flashing blue eyes full of animation. Were they just blue? Were there glints of gray and green? We joked about her eyes, and about how young she was—from which I learned that she had a birthday coming up in a few weeks, on June 11, when she would turn eighteen.

I saw her home to her dorm, and we went our ways for the summer. I had a small, leather-bound volume of Wordsworth that I had picked up at a sale in the University Store. That would do well, I thought. In early June I wrapped it up, suitably inscribed for her birthday, and mailed it to Martha's home address.

She wrote me an acknowledgment, and we exchanged a letter or two while I was in New Hampshire. Then, in September, we were both back in Princeton.

Westminster Choir College was still hard pressed for dormitory space on its small campus. Martha was again lodged in a private home, most of which was leased to the college. In that early fall, I made several trips across town on my bicycle for an evening visit, just to sit with Martha in a corner of the living room or on the front porch of that house on Moore Street.

This was how it came about that one October evening, as we sat in welcoming shadows on the front porch, a subdued light filtering from the living room, Martha began to pour out her intimate feelings. I can't remember just how it went. To me, it was surprising and bewildering. She was telling me how she was sure that she loved me, that I was the one, and the only one, she wanted to be with—always.

I was astounded. Martha was very bright, and she was a leader. Also, while not a rebel, she was quite ready to ignore, or even contravene, social custom, in order to express what she made her own. Had I taken the initiative that evening, saying from my side what she said from hers, that would have been quite according to convention. Why, then, shouldn't the initiative be hers? I don't suggest that her thought went through such steps as these. She simply told me, honestly and freely, what she was thinking and feeling.

In the rush of thought and emotion that was mine, I might have remembered Eloyce and the hurt I may have caused in that situation. Certainly, I was aware of the huge trust that Martha was giving me and how I must not misuse it. I was acutely conscious of the three-and-a-half-year difference in our ages, and the four years in our student careers. She was just eighteen, beginning her sophomore year in college. I was twenty-one, would be twenty-two in January, with a year of graduate study behind me and now entering on my theological program.

Yet we had much in common, and I found her powerfully appealing. Was this love on my side, a love that could be as deep and strong as what she was expressing? Might it be, for me, a wonderful, unexpected gift from God? After some moments, as I can remember it, I said,

"Let's give ourselves some time." (I was definitely the one needing the perspective of time.) "Let's take three days, not seeing or calling each other, just to know our way ahead together."

She agreed. We sat a while longer, then said goodnight. I rode home wondering, feeling dazed.

Through the next morning I moved in the assigned academic pattern, sitting in classes, walking the hallways; but my spirit was absorbed by the decision I needed to make. It would be, if I made it, a commitment for life. That was clear, and it seemed that the choice did not belong to me. The faith tradition I had been born into had become fervently my own, shaped to my thought-system and my personhood. I was sure, now, that I would be given the answer.

Throughout that morning I did not wrestle or agonize in prayer. I pondered and waited. And I found that the answer became clear—quietly, peacefully clear.

In the afternoon I called Martha. Did we need the three days? If she was ready, I would come that same evening. Yes, she said, I should come.

For so great an event of the spirit, there needed to be preparation. As evening came, I was alone in my room. I had a record player, and during the preceding year had become familiar with some favorite compositions. There needed to be music—but first, words.

I opened the Bible to the Book of Genesis, chapter 24—to the charming pastoral idyll that recounts the marriage of Isaac and Rebekah—how Abraham sends his trusted servant back to his home country and his kindred, to find a wife for his son Isaac; how the servant relies on the God of his master, and is led to Rebekah; how her family confers and she declares that she will go with the servant, and how Isaac, walking alone in the evening, sees the camel caravan returning and hears the story, and how he takes Rebekah to be his wife, and loves her.

I read it through, as I had before, and then I put on the phonograph Beethoven's Fifth Symphony—just the Final Movement, that wonderful, solemn, joyously triumphant sound filling my room with its glorious conviction.

That was it. With the music brimming over in my spirit, I went out into a mild, cool October evening, got on my bicycle, and rode across town to Moore Street, to Martha. I told her that I now knew my love for her. We committed ourselves to one another for a long and good life that we believed God had given and would give to us together.

The following day I went to the Princeton University Store and picked out a small gold ring with the Princeton seal. Inside, I had it engraved with our initials and the date, 10-8-40. Martha was so happy when I gave it to her, and she told me later how her parents drove up to Princeton and took her home for the weekend. Her father was at that time serving a Methodist church in Trenton, so they were only a half-hour away.

They, of course, knew about me, but not the news that she had to share. Martha said that they were sitting around the table after dinner, and her sister, Reba, who was eighteen years older than she, was also there. So, Martha just brought out the Princeton ring, which she deliberately had not been wearing, and rolled it across the table to her mother, inviting her to look inside. That dramatic gesture, and Martha's follow-up explanation, as she slipped the ring on her finger, brought tumbling questions and some expressions of concern. Was it wise, and was she prepared to make such a commitment? And what about the difference in age and in preparation between her and me?

But Della and Henry Bradway knew their third child, their youngest. She had grown up, in some ways, like an only child, with Reba eighteen and Matthew twelve years older than she was. And she was bright, always at the top of her class, decided in her opinions, and sure of herself. They knew—and were glad to know—that I also was in the evangelical Christian tradition, although Presbyterian, rather than Methodist. Henry, half playfully, wondered about that, as I, too, would be going into the ministry.

Della's comment, at the end of the extensive conversation, was, "Well, I hope you can keep up with him."

True, at that point, academically, I had quite a lead; but Della didn't need to worry. Martha and I would take our parallel, but separate, paths; each aware of how the other could excel.

*****

Through that fall and winter, we used every opportunity to be together. In the spring, in a simple ceremony in Westminster's dining hall when most of the school was assembled for dinner, we announced our engagement. My parents were in Korea, at their medical mission post in Taegu. I had written them about Martha, telling them my feelings for her, and had heard back, after the usual lag of a week or two. There was airmail service across the Pacific, but it was irregular as yet.

For the upcoming summer I wasn't going to New Hampshire. As I was well into my theological studies, I had an invitation from a church in Phoenixville, outside of Philadelphia, to fill in for a pastor who would be away on a summer leave. I had the run of his family's large, very empty house, and now I had a car. My maternal grandmother had died, leaving to each of her grandchildren a bequest that was enough for me to buy a small, much-used Ford sedan. As my responsibility in Phoenixville was largely confined to Sundays, one week, I took the road to Malaga, in southern New Jersey. There was a Methodist Camp Meeting in Malaga, and Martha's parents had the use of a cottage, with a sleeping arrangement for me. Malaga also has one of the small lakes that dot southern New Jersey, inviting Martha and me to enjoy being beside or in the water.

When the summer had passed, we were back in Princeton, Martha now in her junior year at Westminster. Since the college focused on preparing church musicians, and she had a joint major in choral conducting and organ, she landed a weekend job in a church in Collingswood, some forty miles away. That meant going down on Friday for choir rehearsals, with private voice lessons on Saturday and services on Sunday, before returning home Sunday evening. We agreed that she should use my car, taking with her several fellow students who had jobs at churches in the same area, to share expenses.

The arrangement worked well, except for one time, when Martha was following a pick-up truck with a long board sticking out the back. The board had a proper red flag on the end, but that didn't help when the truck stopped more quickly than Martha could, and the board scraped up my Ford's hood and crashed through the windshield, to within a foot of the face of Martha's front seat passenger. He, unfortunately, was a very excitable young man. My car seemed to have been more easily repaired than his nerves.

This was now the fall of 1941, with war raging in Europe. Letters from my mother and dad in Korea were sporadic and written in very guarded language. Then came December 7, the Japanese surprise attack at Pearl Harbor, Franklin Roosevelt's "Day of Infamy" speech, and the US Declaration of War. The curtain fell on any possible communication of my siblings and me with our parents.

On a different "front," in the spring I got a job. There was a church in northwestern New Jersey whose pastor was taking a leave to enter the Navy as a chaplain. Although not yet ordained, I could serve as "supply" pastor in his absence. This meant regular work—my goal of service to God—and a salary as well. It didn't matter that the salary was modest. The church would pay $25 a week, and there was a church in a nearby town with membership down to only a couple of families, but determined to survive, that offered $5 for a service on Sunday afternoon. Remember, this was 1942, and the dollar went further then.

*****

As you might expect, Martha and I wanted to make wedding plans. Henry and Della had reasonable doubts. Their daughter was still in her junior year in college. If she took this on, would she still go ahead and get her degree? I also had a year to go before finishing at seminary, but that didn't involve them.

It became a primary part of Martha's and my commitment that, if we got married, she would follow through to graduation at Westminster. For my side, there could be no consulting with my parents in Korea about a wedding. We would have waited, if we had known—but the curtain was tightly closed.

We set a wedding date, May 19. That was near the end of the academic year at Westminster, and for our wedding Martha wanted to have her college roommates in her bridal party, before they scattered for the summer. In addition, the seminary would be closing, and I wanted several close friends to take part.

We both believed that our wedding was—and should clearly be—an act of worship. Martha would carry a Bible, bound in white and trailing white ribbons with small white flowers. Her attendants would carry candles. A couple of them protested, but she was firm. They would process down the aisle, carefully, each with a lighted candle, surrounded at the base by a circle of small flowers. Our venue would be the First Presbyterian Church in Princeton, now Nassau Presbyterian in Princeton, which had been important to us in our relationship.

Our wedding itself was simple. The date was close to the end of Westminster's final examination period. In fact, Martha presented herself that morning for her final in English, but the instructor said,

"What are you doing here, on your wedding day? You'll have an A in this course, anyway. Now, go along and get ready for your evening."

On that "evening" the service, which Henry Bradway conducted, moved to a climax when a group from the Westminster Choir, at the close, sang the soaring, poignant "Lutkin Benediction." That richly musical and spiritual anthem, the theme music of Westminster's tradition, filled the shadowy sanctuary, brimming over in our hearts with the serene hope of its message.

Martha and her family had prepared a reception in the social hall of the church—simple and folksy, perhaps, but expressive of who and how we were. Then Stew Robinson, a loyal friend, drove Martha and me to my car, parked two blocks away as a precaution against a prankish "Just Married" being printed with soap on the rear window or a string of tin cans tied to the tail pipe.

With huge but happy relief, we drove for an hour or so to Lake Hopatcong, in the northern part of the state. Without the convenience of online searches in that long-ago time, I had used a state road map to go exploring and, driving slowly among trees along a shore of the lake, had come on, and made a reservation at, a pleasant "tourist home." When we arrived, rather late that evening, our hostess was up and expecting us. She showed us a comfortable room, and we collapsed.

For the three days I had booked, our kind hostess prepared attractive, home-cooked meals. They held no attraction for us. We were both so nervously, emotionally exhausted that we couldn't eat. The house had a rowboat, which we took out one day. We both loved the water, and I was happy to be at the oars, until, abruptly, a spring thunderstorm came up.

Lightning flashed and rain began to pelt us. I searched my brain. What had I heard about how dangerous it might or might not be to be out on the water in a thunderstorm? There was a low bridge over a creek that fed into the lake. I pulled hard for the bridge, and we crouched to get under it. At least, there was protection from the drumbeat of the rain. Happily, such seasonal storms are brief. By the time enough water had accumulated above us to begin to pour through the cracks, the black clouds had passed over. We made a very wet return to our tourist home's dock and a squishy entrance into the front hallway.

The new life we were entering on was wonderful, although with much to learn as we explored it together. Bethlehem Presbyterian Church, "our" church, was a small congregation, mostly of farm people, located two or three miles outside the town of Clinton, among the rolling hills of northwestern New Jersey. The church building was a large, Victorian structure, all wood, including its bell tower. Inside, it seemed cavernous for its few worshipers. We learned, though, that this was the historic church's third building, having been preceded by a smaller brick structure and, before that, an actual log church erected in early Colonial times.

Martha and I teamed up from the start. She was on the organ bench, coaxing music from a limited rank of functioning pipes of the sanctuary's organ. In the pulpit, I felt fine. On throughout my life, when I would be on my feet in front of an audience of any kind, the words would come easily. The difficulty for me, even in that first small church, came after the service, when I stood at the door to speak to the people as they were leaving, and I needed to come up quickly with names or a personal comment or question.

Martha

The manse, or pastor's house, was now ours to use. It was large, a rambling, white clapboard structure on a slope opposite the hill where the church stood. We assembled such second-hand furniture as we could and, with Henry and Della's help, settled in. I had to learn to cope with the lawn, which grew profusely. Fortunately for us, just up a lane that ran past one side of the house, there was a father-and-son farm. The son and his wife were close to us in age. The entire household were staunch members of the church and came to be our invaluable guides to this new rural life. One mental picture I have is of Helen, the young farmer's wife, who was rather petite, perched high on the front of a loaded hay wagon, heavy leather reins in her hands, turning the horses up the lane, as husband John and his father ride above her on top of the hay.

On a Saturday evening soon after we moved in there was a knock on our front door. When we opened it, there were church friends on the porch with a basket. Behind them were the headlights of another car and on down the road more cars, a procession of lights. Soon the house was filling with people, voices, and laughter, and our church friends were piling our kitchen and dining table with all kinds of staples, home-preserved vegetables, and fruit—a pantry shower that would keep us well provided for a long time.

We served Bethlehem Presbyterian Church for that year and one more. With Martha doing her final year at Westminster and I at Princeton Seminary, we lived with her parents in Trenton during the week, commuting to Princeton, and went up to our church home each weekend. After graduation I was ordained. The pastor of Bethlehem Church had decided to resign, so I was called as the "installed" pastor. We kept up our weekday commuting pattern. Martha went on at Westminster to earn a master's degree in musicology, while I resumed graduate study, part-time, in English at Princeton.

Let me go back, though, to a scene from our first year at Bethlehem Presbyterian. It is Christmas morning, and I am called for a pastoral emergency. It isn't for a member of the church, but there is some connection with the church, and I need to go.

When I arrive at a suburban house, a small group of family and friends is gathered in the living room. I am drawn aside and told what had happened. In the pre-dawn darkness, the young husband and father of the house had shot himself. The police and coroner had been there and done their parts. Now the young widow sits, dazed and silent in the living room as her two-year-old son plays on the floor. I enter the room to speak to her, then to sit with the others. The husband had no active church affiliation, nor did the wife; but the family had said I should be called.

What do I say? The little boy is trying to play with a partly-put-together toy firetruck. His mother comments that his father would have finished assembling it for him. Since it is Christmas morning, I open the Bible and read from Luke's Nativity narrative. These are words written out of a tradition of faith, for people of faith. What can I, with integrity, say in this present time and place? I offer a prayer.

When I stop, the silence engulfs me. I sit a little longer but can find no right words in my head. I feel the stark pain of this domestic tragedy must not be met with pat assurances, with trite words that will ring hollow. Have I stayed long enough? I get up, say a few words to the young widow, pat her son on the head, and leave.

"Lord God, I've failed. What might I have done? How might I have helped to bring your wise compassion, your gracious presence, into that desolate room?"

I drive home, almost unseeingly, with a wrenching pain in my heart.

*****

One last hurdle remained, for me to complete my PhD: the final oral examination. The graduate division of Princeton's English Department had the use, at that time, of an isolated pair of rooms in the old, Neo-Gothic library. They were reached through a doorway, then down five or six wide stone steps, to a landing with a never-opened oak door to the outdoors; the two rooms stood one on each side. On this afternoon in early May 1945, the faculty committee assembled in one of the rooms to conduct my final oral exam, while I waited in the other. When they called me in, I stood at one side, while they were seated informally around the other.

The first part of the examination was a sort of mock lecture. In the morning I had been given a list of three topics. I was to choose one and use about three hours to prepare a lecture, such as I might give to a sophomore or junior class in college English. This was naturally daunting, but my public speaking experience stood by me. The lecture seemed to go well. After six or seven minutes, the presiding professor interrupted it, with thanks, in order to proceed.

The rest of the examination was free question and response. Any examiner could ask any question he chose, on any period or any work in English and American literature. Of course, the candidate was not expected to match all of the specialists in that room, nor their years of study and research. The test was to see how well he could hold his own in a college classroom or informal discussion. This was a lot harder for me. I am a careful, but slow, reader. Ranging across literature in English, my reading had been spotty and quite thin. The questioners were courteous, but their probing was thorough. Among them, Professor Hubler, a younger department member and an Elizabethan specialist, was relentless. With his questions on non-Shakespearian plays and playwrights of that period, he pinned me to the wall.

At last, the chairman ended the questioning and I was excused, while the committee deliberated. I sat in the opposite room and waited. The oak door of the examining room was firmly closed so that I could hear only a faint murmur of voices that were kept low. The discussion appeared to go on at length and the sun was moving well into the western sky, coming in through small panes in the leaded casements. In my many years of schooling and academic experience, I had never been in doubt about passing an examination, there had of course been disappointments, issues of stronger or weaker performance, but no question of not passing.

Finally, chairs were being pushed back in the other room. The door opened and there were voices and a sound of feet going up the stone steps. I stayed back, out of direct view, feeling that I should wait to be called.

It was after the others had left that the two department members whom I particularly knew and trusted came to the door of the room where I was waiting. They were Prof. Albert Elsasser (Anglo-Saxon specialist) and Prof. Robert Cawley (Victorian era). In their kind, informal way, they told me what I could well surmise, that the committee had rejected my performance on the oral examination. What now to do? They sat down, one on each side of me, on the slate-stone steps.

Cawley knew something of my plans—that Martha and I had been accepted by the Presbyterian Board of Foreign Missions and were under appointment for service in Latin America. I confirmed that, adding that we were due to leave in three weeks, going to Colombia for language study, then on to Chile.

How long would we be gone? I said that the first term of service would be five years; but I also said that, because of the exam, I could ask for a deferment. I felt sure that the mission board, which had already granted us an extension so that I could finish my degree, would allow a further extension, half a year or so, for me to prepare and to come up again for the final oral.

"No," Cawley said. "Go on with the plan you and your wife now have. Carry out your intended mission for these five years, which will pass quickly."

Elsasser added, "And use as much time as you can spare to widen your reading in English literature—to fill in the gaps that you recognize. Then, when you come back and are ready, you can stand before the examining committee again."

There was more talk along those lines. The western light was making jewels of some chips of colored glass in the barred oak doors that shut away the campus springtime outside. I knew that Cawley and Elsasser were right. How might it be, in five years? Elsasser was the older, his craggy face seeming to fit with the Old English texts that he unfolded. Would he be here, in five or six years, if I stood for another examination? And how changed might I be? Who could say?

I felt satisfied this was the right course, and grateful for their encouragement, as we got to our feet in that sterile-seeming, academic setting. They gave me their hands warmly. It was my pledge to myself and to them.

10

Medellín and Mountains of the Moon

She was a vision of delight, standing there in the rich sunlight, with her jaunty pose and her knee-length, flowered skirt, short socks and sandals. The vision, as I squinted through my camera finder, was like that other, earlier vision on that evening of our decisive date at Princeton's McCarter Theater, just over six years earlier.

But this was Medellín, Colombia. Martha was standing in the unpaved street in front of "our" house—the rented one assigned to us by the Spanish Language School. We had been sent there by the Presbyterian Church's Board of Foreign Missions. Martha felt she was on an adventure. She had never been outside the United States. Now we were both commissioned, husband and wife, to serve in Chile under the Presbyterian board. Neither of us spoke Spanish, so that meant a stay of some months in the language school in Medellín, before we moved south to our posting.

It was 1945. We had been in Washington on that April day, at the back of the crowd, trying to catch a glimpse of the caisson carrying the body of President Franklin Roosevelt.

Shortly after that, we rode a train to Miami, where we were roused in pre-dawn dark in our hotel room, and to board our PanAmerican airliner, and saw the day break over the Caribbean.

The aura of adventure carried over when the plane left us on the Colombian coast in tropical Barranquilla. I, of course, had spent years abroad, but all of *this* was new: the colors and odors of tropical fruits and the steamy air that conveyed them; the staccato noise of voices haggling in the street market right beside the rather informal airport building. To Martha, as a native New Jersey girl, it had to be even more exotic.

We boarded a smaller, Colombian plane, and were treated to a spectacular flight. Aloft, we were quickly over mountain ridges. Huge thunderclouds hung in the air, and our pilot weaved around them—and right through some. Outside our window were intervals of blindness caused by thick vapor, breaking out to startling views of close, bright hilltops and of deep, green gorges between them.

At length, abruptly, we were descending, coming down past densely green mountain sides, to land on the Medellín airfield. The air, as we disembarked, was mild and bright, redolent with the freshness of a recent rain. This was May; but when we left, half a year later in November, it would still seem like spring at this moderate elevation not very far north of the Equator.

We were met by the director of the language school, a former missionary to Japan. He and his wife, who became something like foster parents to us during our months in Medellín, had been forced by the war to relocate, and the mission board had assigned them to this position, requiring adjustment to a new language and lifestyle. We were there when, a few weeks later, the news of Hiroshima came and, shortly thereafter, V-J Day. For our "foster parents," there were tears: joy and hope all mixed up with anxiety for the Japanese people.

The Spanish Language School was a large former residence. On the wall that framed a second-floor balcony grew a luxuriant bougainvillea loaded with brilliant yellow flowers. In Medellín flowers were everywhere. Natural life was close and abundant.

When the director was showing us the house where we would be living, Martha went over to a shuttered window of our bedroom to see the view. As she opened the shutter, a cow, browsing grass at the street's edge just outside, raised its large, moist mouth, almost touching her. There was no glass in the windows, only an iron grill, and the dining and sitting rooms, and also the kitchen, had no wall on the side toward the central patio, which in turn was open to the sky. One counted, year-round, on the benevolent climate, including almost daily rain showers; generally brief.

We found that the abundant life included large cockroaches. It was not a good idea to go into the kitchen barefoot at night, nor any place else, for that matter. Some people had a kitchen table with each leg standing in a pan of kerosene. There were other precautions to be taken for food preparation and storage. The language school had arranged for the services of a cook, a jolly, matronly woman who had with her a somewhat shy daughter, about seven.

At first, we shared our house with Linda, a missionary nurse who was finishing her Spanish course, leaving shortly to take up her assignment in a mountain town in another part of the country. On our second day, we came upon Linda in her room, sitting by the open window, chatting through the grill with a group of children gathered on the street side. How impossible it seemed to us! Could we ever arrive at such fluency in the language?

The grammarian of the school, Prof. Irégui (ih-RAY-guee) favored classical Castilian Spanish, including use of the *theta*. This means sounding the letter *z*, in Spanish, as a soft *th* in English. Latin Americans generally sound it as *s*, as in *raíz* (ra-EES), rather than (ra-EETH). Prof. Irégui was courteous, in an old-school way, and patient. He could be demanding but managed it in a gentlemanly fashion.

On the other hand, we had a pronunciation teacher, Sr. Iriarte (ih-ree-AR-tay, with r's lightly rolled), who could be merciless. Most of us realized, in retrospect, that we owed much to him. It was very important, for our work, that we learn to speak the language, not only correctly but also with as little foreign accent as possible. One of Iriarte's teaching tools was to mimic his students: after he had asked the student to pronounce a word or phrase, he would imitate the response as it sounded to him. He would repeat, in exaggerated style, the flat *gringo* accent of the hapless student.

It was hard for us learners to be ridiculed, even when we knew that he likely was right. Women students, in particular, would sometimes leave an Iriarte session in tears. Martha, as a trained vocal musician, seemed to get the pronunciation well, and I worked at it diligently. Later on, when I had a weekly radio program, it was supremely gratifying if I met a chance listener who said, "Oh, was that you on the radio? I didn't realize it was a North American."

The months in Medellín slipped away. It was great to be immersed every day in the language and life of the people. On one break we hiked up a road in the mountains—most of Colombia is mountains, mantled in green in that latitude. The wrinkles in the Earth's surface that run from the bottom of South America northward, forming the Andes, split into three ranges in Colombia. Then they coalesce, continuing through Central America and Mexico, and the American and Canadian Rockies, finally twisting west in Alaska's Aleutian Islands, to reach toward Siberia.

As that December of 1945 approached, although we were far from having mastered Spanish, we had a good grounding and needed to get on to Chile. We had met, in Princeton, a missionary couple, Dorothy and Reed Edwards, who were on furlough. Now they were back in Antofagasta, the chief seaport in northern Chile, and they invited us to stop there when we arrived in the country. The turn of the year comes in early summer in the Southern Hemisphere, so that was when both the Presbyterian Mission in Chile and the national church's Presbytery of Chile held their annual meetings.

In Antofagasta, Reed Edwards helped us through customs and drove us around in the mission auto, to get acquainted with the small city and its setting. When one flies southward from tropical-green, verdant Colombia, as we had done, over equally green Ecuador and the northern coast of Peru, where it bulges westward into the Pacific Ocean, the plane reaches a region where the outline of the bulge is rounding east again toward the mass of the continent. There the cool Humboldt Current, which has been flowing northward from the Antarctic, along the whole western side of South America, is diverted into the open Pacific. Seen from the air, the effect is dramatic. It appears as if a gigantic line had been drawn across the landscape eastward, as far as the eye can see. The moist, tropical green, extending down from the north, stops abruptly at that line. From there, to the south, the tawny brown of desert begins.

That desert is the creation of the Humboldt Current. Even into the subtropics, the current keeps the ocean cooler than the land. The result is that when moisture-laden clouds roll in off the ocean and meet the warm landmass, they simply rise and dissipate, dropping no rain. There is some rain or snow in the high mountains, forming widely scattered streams that reach or almost reach the ocean, and that form valley oases of greenery. Northern Chile is more arid, featuring the awesome Atacama Desert. Towns and small cities, like Arica, Iquique, Tocopilla, and Antofagasta itself, must pipe most or all of their water from the high Andes.

Reed drove us up to where a dry ravine opened out onto the desert. He pulled over and we got out. The ground under our feet, hard and dry, stretched away to low hills. There were ridges and hollows, a distant, undulating landscape, but all was in tones of brown and gray.

We drove on for perhaps a mile, to the top of a low rise, where we got out again. From where we stood, the pale ribbon of the unpaved road ran ahead and behind us—no vehicle in sight. The landscape was empty, windless and still. There was no twitter of birds—not even the whirr of an insect or faint scuttle of a beetle—no life, and no sound whatever.

"Listen," Reed said; "be quiet and listen."

This was total, absolute silence. I felt as if I could hear my stifled breathing and the beating of my heart. I had never, anywhere, experienced such awesome silence. In its austerity, its lifelessness, Chile's Atacama Desert is like the mountains of the Moon.

We had a brief, but pleasant, visit with the Edwards in Antofagasta. Then all of us headed south to Santiago for the mission and Presbytery annual meetings. Dorothy had booked a flight, but we two and Reed took the narrow-gauge train—two days and nights to cover some nine hundred miles.

11

Going North

WE SAT ACROSS FROM each other at a dilapidated metal table in the railroad station waiting room. The large room was nearly empty; the air rather close and muggy; but between trains it was a good enough place for our talk. The date was late January 1947, mid-summer in Valparaíso, Chile, deep in the Southern Hemisphere.

Martha and I sat on one side of the table, across from Pastor Ortega. Our table positions were symbolic. Pastor of the downtown First Presbyterian Church of Valparaíso, the Reverend Jaime Ortega was also, that year, Moderator of the Presbytery of Chile. Could we get across to him what we urgently needed to communicate, and would he concur with our request?

There was history behind this meeting. It was our own recent history, but, also, some decades of Presbyterian history in Chile, a history of which we had been made acutely aware. Our mission assignment, for our first year in Chile, was to live in Santiago, work on improving our grasp of the Spanish language, learn something of the background and culture of the people, and perhaps take first steps toward outreach among university students.

Our longer-term assignment seemed clear to the Mission. James Maclaine, a scholarly veteran missionary, had recently retired and left the country. With a doctorate in English literature, he had secured a position and reputation on the faculty of the University of Chile, in Santiago. I had nearly completed a PhD in English at Princeton; so, the logic was that I might step into Maclaine's shoes. I didn't, personally, wish to make a career of teaching at the university, even if that could be arranged. It didn't fit with my idea of missionary outreach. But if Martha and I could establish some kind of center to which we could draw university students, relate to them, and communicate a message of a vital, personal Christian faith, that would be a direct, satisfying mission assignment.

As our first year in Santiago, 1946, unfolded, we put out feelers about our university idea, but with little success. At the same time, we began to be aware that there was a deep, sometimes bitter cleft between the mission, on one side, and the national church leadership on the other. Put bluntly, Presbyterian mission policy in Chile, as well as in some other parts of the world, had a distinctly "colonial" aspect. In Chile this was more acute because the national church was small. The Presbytery of Chile comprised fewer than two dozen congregations, many of them too modest in size to afford a pastor, even at the minimal salary on which most of the pastors and their families were expected to survive.

By contrast, the mission maintained institutions: an elementary and secondary school in Valparaíso; a small maternity hospital and a large, prestigious boys' academy in Santiago; and some lesser enterprises. These institutions were supervised by missionaries and sustained as needed by funds from the United States, which the Chile mission dispersed. Certainly, there were some missionaries who worked in the churches; and, in the Presbyterian system, missionaries who were ordained clergy were voting members of the presbytery; but all Presbyterian missionaries in Chile constituted the Chile mission, and the mission controlled its members and their assignments, its institutions, and all funds received from the New York Board of Foreign Missions.

During our year in Santiago, Martha and I were introduced to this bipolar situation. Then, abruptly, we were at the center of it. The leadership of the presbytery knew that the Chile mission would be giving us a specific assignment, and they seemingly decided to make of us a test case. They gave the mission secretary an ultimatum: "We want the Fletchers assigned to Vallenar, or to no location in Chile."

Vallenar. Our narrow-gauge train had stopped there, briefly, on our two-day ride south from Antofagasta almost a year earlier. We knew the town existed thanks to one of the few small rivers fed by the snows of the Andes that managed to survive crossing the scorching North Chilean desert to the sea. Its narrow valley had a thin ribbon of green from the mountains to the ocean, and in the middle was a dusty town, Vallenar. There was a church there, but presently no pastor; hence the presbytery's decision.

We said that we would go to see it, taking the mission car. Our friends Dorothy and Reed Edwards had been transferred south from Antofagasta, and the car was available.

It was a long drive. Rolling out of Santiago in early morning, we left Chile's fertile Central Valley, labored over and around low mountains, and watched the countryside progressively grow dry and parched. The long summer day was ending when we approached the valley of the Huasco River. One comes to it abruptly, seeing the road bend and take a steep, improbable plunge to the valley floor. The stream glimmered along one side of a level area massed with gray-brown, corrugated iron roofs, a few new enough to catch a glistening light.

The church building, when we got to it, had a plain, mud-plastered front, with a sun-weathered wood door and a small window on each side. Paint was sparse, but the overall presentation, on the unpaved street, was tidy. The property was cared for, as we learned, by a church family next door, who received us graciously into their home. They had prepared a guest room for us. There was a bed, not very wide but appealing, after our long car trip. It had an embroidered coverlet, and a single bare bulb hung from the ceiling above it.

We were glad to turn in as early as we could, settling gratefully, close together, in the narrow bed. The light was a problem. Martha always hated to have total darkness at night, but the one bulb was either on or off. When I switched it off, there was only the faintest glimmer filtering in from outside. Then, after a few minutes, came a scratch overhead—more scratches, some squeaking and scurrying.

Martha clutched me. "The light; get the light on!"

Our movement and light had effect. The scurrying stopped, at least for a while. I knew that the light had to stay on. We had to get some sleep, however we managed it.

In the morning we drove around to see the town. I was watching Martha. During our year in Santiago, she had begun to show signs of nervous tension and psychological stress. Now it was plain that, with the succession of drab, dirt streets and dusty, meager storefronts, her mood was darkening.

We had a note introducing us to Anita, the daughter of a missionary couple in Santiago who had married a British Chilean. They owned a *finca*, a farm, down the valley, toward the sea. We took the road out of town, and things improved. Careful use of water from the stream nourished green fields and pastures. There were sheep, goats, and some cattle. When we came to the *finca* of Anita and her husband, we were pleased to see a neat fence and gate, a small sweep of lawn and flowers. Anita received us warmly. Her husband was away and would be back later, but she treated us to a delicious lunch, served in their gracious, airy dining room. There was coffee with real cream. I was happy to see how Martha brightened and to hear the spirit in her voice again.

Back in our car, the road soon brought us to a port. There was a jetty and a cluster of fishing houses, with some boats pulled up on a stony beach. The nearest house looked like it had been made of driftwood. Martha wanted to stop again at Anita's *finca*, but I said that it was getting along toward tea time and that would be awkward. Besides, I was to lead a service at the little church that evening and needed to get back.

Several days later, again in Santiago, we reported to the mission executive committee, which was in session. Vallenar, we said, was impossible—out of the question.

In my private thought, I would have attempted it, if that was the assignment we were given, and if that was how we could contribute to the work of the church. I had grown up in a missionary family. But I could see that it could not work for Martha, especially as nervous as she was at that time.

The committee listened; they conferred and said, "We're sorry. We'd like to help; but there's nothing we can do. You'll have to work out your assignment with the presbytery."

So that was what had brought us from Santiago, on that late January day in 1947, to the railroad station in Valparaíso, to sit across from Pastor Ortega at a creaky metal table. As the moderator, he was the chief executive officer of the presbytery, which was the governing body of all of the Presbyterian clergy and congregations in Chile.

He had offered nothing better, as a place to meet, than the drafty railroad station. We had a plan. I had come up with an idea and tried it out with Martha, and she had agreed. We could both hark back, a bit more than a year, to our first arrival on Chilean soil and the Edwards introducing us to Antofagasta.

I assured Pastor Ortega, and through him the presbytery, that we had no desire to remain in Santiago. We agreed that work with university students was not presently indicated, nor was it what we wished to do. We would go north to serve the church in Chile. But why just to Vallenar? We would go on, all the way to Antofagasta, the chief city of the whole northern region of the country, but with no Presbyterian church. We would undertake to plant one there.

The negotiation was successful. Pastor Ortega was persuaded and through him the presbytery leadership. Some four weeks later, with our few goods packed to be shipped, we were again in the mission car, driving northward. This time, the car was assigned to us and our destination was nearly a thousand road miles away.

*****

Let me add here one more scene. It comes some ten months later, after we had established ourselves and begun our work there. Although we didn't suspect it at the time, it turned out that while we hammered out those miles, much of it on a rough, single-lane dirt road crossing the Chilean north, Martha was pregnant. Happily, all went well. Some eight months after our long trip north, we flew back to Santiago to be near our trusted friend Marie Schultz, RN, and the *Madre-e-Hijo* (Mother-and-Child) Presbyterian maternity hospital.

Because of some minor complications, Martha was still in Santiago, after baby Donna's birth, and I with her, when the annual meeting of the presbytery opened in early January. I went to the meeting, which lasted late into the evening, and when I got back Martha had long been in bed. I bent over her, dangling in her face something that I was wearing on a ribbon around my neck.

"Guess who is the new moderator of Presbytery" I asked exultantly. "*I* am, and here's the medallion that is passed along, given to the moderator to wear!"

Less than a year after the presbytery's ultimatum, our trip to Vallenar, and our negotiation with Pastor Ortega, I was elected; the first missionary in many years elected by the presbytery of Chile to the moderator position. Here was a plain, profound lesson in mission/church relations, in deep-rooted national/foreign antagonism, and how it can be resolved.

12

"Oasis of the Soul"

THE RADIO STATION AT Antofagasta turned out to be a fragile-looking frame structure set on a bare slope, close beside the radio's angle-iron transmitting tower. When we reached it in low gear, via a hilly, switch-back road and stepped out of the car, there was a fine view across the roofs of the city below and the harbor. The brazen sky was cloudless; the Pacific, a deep blue; the ground under our feet, a hard, unyielding crust, as it would always be.

We were there, Martha and I, on a pioneering missionary venture, as agreed in our negotiation with the presbytery. The venture: to open a center and establish a new church. We had one entering wedge—just one—a letter to a judge in the city who was a graduate of the prestigious Presbyterian boys' academy in Santiago and who might support our effort.

He was just that. He gave us an introduction to the owner of the city's one radio station, and the owner gave us a fifteen-minute slot on Sundays, at noon. We said we'd call it *La Hora Presbiteriana*, The Presbyterian Hour, because we wanted the name of our project, *Presbiteriana*, to begin to be known.

We had a folding, portable Estey organ, the type with pedals and bellows that a few of you may have known. To our pleasure, we found that when Martha sat pumping it and singing into a microphone, the sound came over the airwaves remarkably well. I did the speaking, introducing the program and Martha's music, and adding a brief message each week.

We weighed the content of our quarter-hour program carefully, wanting it to get known as an interlude, both pleasant and uplifting.

After a few months, feeling that the Presbyterian name had been aired enough, we changed the title of our program to *Oasis del Alma*, Oasis of the Soul. The first word was intended to convey the sort of refreshing interlude we wanted listeners to experience, in that arid, desert setting.

For our first months in Antofagasta, we rented a house in a newly developed area on the southern edge of the city. The house was right on the shore, so literally that the outdoor patio had a long, walled yard in back, that sloped almost to the sea-mossed stones washed by the Pacific at high tide.

As an early venture, and to begin to draw together members of the four or five Presbyterian congregations scattered across the region, we sent out a call for a "youth congress." About a dozen young people—teens and early twenties—responded, coming by bus for our two-day conference. We had no property except our rented house; but that would serve. We had advertised the gathering as a "camp," and these young people were used to making do with little. The girls squeezed into the second bedroom, and the boys camped on the back patio. Martha was pregnant with Donna, whose birth in Santiago I already recounted, but she managed the meal planning, cooking, and coordination of kitchen tasks, true to the New Jersey camp-meeting tradition of her Methodist upbringing.

Our closing service was memorable, under the night sky on our long back patio, where the boys had built a fire that crackled, as the waves lapped only ten yards away. Emotions flowed. These earnest young Protestant Christians, used to being few in number, drew close together and pledged to support one another, as we two did, also.

After half a year, we moved to a two-story building closer to the city center. The ground floor had a wide entrance and a single long room designed for use as a store. We furnished it to serve as a youth center, including, at one side, short pews to form a chapel. Upstairs was an apartment, quite sufficient for our family of two with a third member on the way.

On Sunday evenings, as announced on our radio program, we began to hold worship services in the first-floor chapel. Martha sat at the organ and I stood behind a podium/pulpit. On the first Sunday, only one person came, a small woman, middle aged, dressed in black, with a black shawl drawn over her head. Zulema de Anastasi was her name. The next week she was back, our congregation of one.

"Oasis of the Soul"

After the service, Sra. Zulema said, "This is what I have longed for all my life. I was baptized and married by the Church (meaning, naturally, the Roman Catholic Church). I have attended and obeyed. But here there is warmth. There is a message that reaches me in my heart. Can I belong here?"

Sra. Zulema had no children, but she soon brought her niece to our service and, in time, her husband, as well as others of her extended family. And some young people were drawn to the youth center. After two years we had a nucleus—twenty-six—who had knelt to be baptized. I told them that, as they had been baptized in infancy, our Presbyterian teaching would accept that; but they said, no, this was now their choice, their faith, and they wanted to express and confirm it by baptism.

That January of 1949, at its annual meeting, the presbytery voted enthusiastically to give formal organization, in Antofagasta, to the Presbyterian Church of Christ the King. It was a name I had proposed, an affirmation of our loyalty and dedication.

At that same time, we were in negotiation for a permanent site. The Presbyterian boys' academy in Santiago had been shut down and its valuable property sold. This followed a protracted conflict, including the ousting of more than one director and student protests. The Mission Board in New York, the academy's legal owner, designated a part of the proceeds to be used for church work in Chile. We in Antofagasta were able to buy the *Quinta Casale*. *Quinta* (KEEN-tah) in this case meant a green-vegetable farm, which occupied two-thirds of a city block—part of it irrigated with scant city water, to grow lettuce and other choice vegetables. The property's name and reputation, however, stemmed from the other part, a restaurant known as a rendezvous for the city's business elite for the making and breaking of sometimes dubious deals.

"So, you're buying the Quinta Casale for your church," one of my friends remarked. "You'll have to sprinkle a lot of holy water around that place!"

*****

Martha was far advanced in her second pregnancy. This time, with the January meetings of the presbytery and mission passed—her due date was early April—and with Antofagasta now definitely our home, Martha felt decided about having the delivery there, even though the city's hospital was a rambling, Spanish-colonial structure offering rather primitive facilities. She did have a good obstetrician, a Yugoslav Chilean in whom she trusted.

In late March, however, he told her that he must go to an important professional conference in Brazil. It was all right. He was sharing all her medical information with a midwife in whom he had complete confidence and who would take excellent care of her, should the delivery come along before he got back.

On the morning of April first it did. The signs were unmistakable. The midwife came and agreed that we should get Martha to the hospital, and soon. We helped her into the car, and little Donna, too, as we didn't feel that we could leave her with a household helper whom we had.

The Antofagasta hospital had no obstetric facility, as such. Martha was accommodated in a private room, one in a series built in a row under a long, tiled roof. Each room had only one access, a door that opened onto a long, paved patio under the sky. There, the midwife made Martha as comfortable as possible, while two-year-old Donna and I took up our vigil on a bench among some potted ferns, outside. This was a new adventure for Donna, and with her happy disposition, she skipped around while we waited, and time slowly passed.

The shadows of the taller ferns crept across the paving stones, while I kept listening. I could hear muffled voices, but no words. The midwife came once to the door to give me encouragement. Then, abruptly, after the voices stopped, out of the silence came a thin, unmistakable cry. I hugged Donna and she hugged me back.

"That's your baby brother or sister," I said. Did she understand what that meant, and would mean, for her? Not likely; but she knew it was happy news.

When we could see Martha, she was wan, but radiant, holding our second baby girl. We named her Sylvia, not for anyone in either family, but because we liked the name and it worked equally well in Spanish and English.

*****

Martha and I had a furlough coming up. Our first five-year term was finishing, and we would be in the United States for a year of R and R, study, and to promote the mission cause among as many local churches as we could reach. Meanwhile, the Antofagasta project we had started was at a critical stage, such that the Chile mission transferred a couple, the Fisks, from their assignment in the south to carry forward the work for that year.

I knew Paul Fisk from Princeton Seminary days. He was two years ahead of me, known in our eating club for his blond California good looks, his vigorous lifestyle, and genial optimism. Now, he and Priscilla chose to make the trip north by coastal steamer, with their two-year-old son, David. They were just back from furlough, with new childcare equipment and other items that they had not even unpacked.

Martha and I went to meet their boat, leaving little Donna in care of our trusted, home helper, who in those days was called a "maid." Martha had her second baby, three-week-old Sylvia, in her arms. The ship was in, but at our approach to the dock area, we were stopped by a guard. There was some problem with the ship. We sat in the car and waited, then waited some more. The guard disappeared, then finally came back with news: a passenger on the ship was sick, a *gringo*, he thought, and the authorities were detaining everyone in temporary quarantine.

The *gringo* would be Paul. I said to Martha, "I'll take you and the baby home, and come back alone to see what I can do."

We had rented a house for the Fisks—a good location backing up on the new church property, which put it a few blocks from our apartment. Back at the dock, I confirmed that the sick passenger was Paul. I managed to see him, with Priscilla and David, and to arranged for all three to be transferred to the rented house. Paul had been running a high fever for most of the four days of their voyage, prostrate on his bunk in the suffocating air of a tiny cabin, with a porthole that couldn't be opened. The tentative medical diagnosis was polio, although in northern Chile there was no experience with polio—only dread.

In the house, Paul's condition appeared to be deteriorating. His feet and lower legs already were going numb. An ambulance moved him to the hospital, to an isolation unit. I was with him there, and he took my hand weakly.

"Stay with me," he said; but I told him I had to go to see the US consul.

In those days the critical resource for acutely ill polio patients was the iron lung, a device with an enclosed chamber in which air pressure could be alternately applied and released, to keep patients breathing when their lungs failed. We knew there was none in Antofagasta. The US consul contacted the embassy in Santiago—no iron lung in any hospital there either, nor in any nearby country. The embassy would try to arrange an emergency flight to the United States. I returned to the Antofagasta hospital—to be told that the patient had died.

I got that word to the consul, then enlisted a doctor friend who lived across the street from us to go with me to the rented house, to tell Priscilla. It would be crushing news for her. Spanish had been her parents' first language growing up in the American Southwest. She clung, sobbing, to the doctor for several long minutes before managing to regain her composure.

The authorities were insisting that Priscilla and little David must remain quarantined in that house, and only I would be permitted to come and go, as their outside contact. That evening, and each evening, I took them part of the dinner Martha prepared, using a Chilean-style stack of pans with a handle. It tore the heart, to see how bare and cheerless the house was—just trunks and boxes and a couple of chairs, for David to play among. Priscilla didn't want to unpack, not knowing what they would do next.

On the second evening following Paul's death, as I was trying to find words of reassurance, Priscilla suddenly embraced and clung to me, sobbing, as she had done with our doctor friend; then, just as suddenly, she stood back, saying, "Thank you for coming" and let me leave.

As I walked home down the sloping street, I said aloud, "Lord, you have made me be a tower of strength!" It was an odd, self-important thought, but I meant to express sincerely my gratitude—that, even with all my innate reticence, I could be a refuge and source of strength to another being.

The US consul had told me that when he got the word to Santiago that Paul had died, there was a special plane already on the tarmac, prepared for the flight to Antofagasta, then on to the United States. Now, with the consul's help, I arranged for Paul's body to be embalmed, in preparation for a different return to his homeland. Then Priscilla, consulting with Paul's parents in California, decided that his body should remain in Chile, the land to which Paul had wanted to devote his life. With her concurrence, I planned a simple service, to be held in the city cemetery once her quarantine was lifted.

Our church's members were there, including some of the youth group. The cemetery is above ground—long rows of concrete niches, four or five high, each sealed with a slab, appropriately inscribed. There is no greenery, no flowers, no grass, even; just the timeless austerity of that desert location.

"Oasis of the Soul"

When Paul's plain coffin had been pushed into its niche and I had read some appropriate passages from the Bible, I offered a simple message, how our high purposes may be left unrealized, as it seems; but it is God, the Inspirer of those purposes, who gives fulfillment in God's way and in God's timelessness, as we were there to witness and to believe.

As the mason sealed up the slab securing Paul's niche, I lifted my gaze to the outline of those rainless hills above the city. I thought of Paul's embalmed body, lying in that dry place year after year, still appearing young and fit, while I would be growing old, long after that.

*****

A couple, recently stationed in a small seaport to the north of ours, was temporarily transferred to cover the Antofagasta project. Priscilla and David boarded, with us, one of the Grace Line freight/passenger ships bound for New York.

Standing at the stern rail, we watched the outline of the drab city and its hills, that had grown home-like, dwindle and then fade. God willing, we would be back again.

13

Communism and a Lecture on Melville

WHEN WE WERE AGAIN in the United States, the mission board put before me a proposal to join for half a year a study group on a Christian approach to Communism. That was a timely topic in 1950. I explained that, along with the promotional work for our mission in Chile, which I would expect to be doing, I needed to use my furlough year to prepare for a re-take of the Final Oral in English at Princeton. The board agreed to this, if I would join the Communism study.

Our family had the use, for that year, of one of the Payne Hall apartments in Princeton. The Communism study meant, for me, commuting to New York, where most of our group of seven or eight were located. There were two of us in Princeton, riding the train each day that a session was held. Brad (Bradford) and his family were on furlough from Brazil, as I recall, and we were glad to have each other's company.

I found the study stimulating and rewarding. The associations and the activities together were enjoyable; even while close-up exploration of world Communism as it was at that time could be intense, almost unnerving. Among our group of students, we agreed to maintain a non-committal attitude as we learned as much as we could about the stance of Communism—its tenets, current programs, and prospects in the world, and its impact on Christian thought and action. We listened to speakers, some attacking and some radically advocating Communist ideas and ideals. And we tried to digest our findings, partly by vigorous discussion within our group.

Communism and a Lecture on Melville

Some of us wrote responses. I naturally took a hand in that; and, in a later stage of the study, some of us were delegated to produce what became a mission board publication: *A Christian Approach to Communism*.

In all of this, the fresh and concentrated focus was exciting to me. Our recent years in Chile had also been tightly focused, but on a local scene of rather narrow scope. In this study, the scope and implications were worldwide. Brad and I talked about that, riding the elevated rails that cross New Jersey's swampy flatland across from New York City, exchanging reactions and comments on what we had been reading and hearing, and how it might relate to faith and action in the countries where we had committed ourselves to serve.

After the Communism study finished, I was able to secure a private cubicle, ideally situated in the bowels of Princeton University's new Firestone Library. We were now a family, with our first two daughters, both born in Chile, and quite soon, a third child to join the group. It was getting to be a good deal to handle, and in my library hideaway, as my needs and duties at home permitted, I could concentrate on reading, oblivious to day and night, time and season, even crying children.

There were opportunities for promotional work. Invitations would come along for visits to churches or church groups. Sometimes the invitation was for Martha as well as me, and we would go as a family, which could be difficult but effective. We would remember one such visit, when all four of us went.

My presentation was always better if Martha shared in it, and this time, since we knew some of the church members, we felt that Donna was old enough to take a part. Our hostess assured us that the younger Sylvia would be fine, in her care. The meeting went quite long, as they generally did, and our return to our hosts' home was further delayed by a summer thunderstorm.

When we got to the house, we found that our hostess had put eleven-month-old Sylvia down for a nap in a quiet bedroom. Sylvia was seemingly fine with that arrangement—until the storm broke, with lightning and thunder. When we went into the bedroom, she was standing in a corner of the crib, soaked with vomit. She had registered her protest in a very effective way. We learned, afterward, that she could protest in that same devastating way if felt pushed to her extreme.

My re-take of the final oral examination in English was scheduled in October of that year, 1951. Our third child, who turned out to be our son Tommy, arrived in August. We were by then staying provisionally with Martha's parents, before our return to Chile at the end of the month. Baby Tommy was afflicted with colic. Perhaps it was because his mother, who was nursing him, was in all probability suffering as much as the child. In effect, Tommy had to be held and walked for long stretches, night as well as day, as he twisted and cried with pain. Martha and I divided the nightly care, taking shifts. If Tommy broke out crying on her shift, she would get up to try to comfort him; if the disruption occurred on my shift, I was the one. We managed the best way we could as, inexorably, my exam day approached.

Finally, I stood again before the English Department's Graduate Committee. Many of the faces had changed. Elsasser had retired; but Cawley was still there. I chose, for my sample lecture, a topic on Herman Melville (*Moby Dick*)—and learned afterward from Robert Cawley that one of the new faculty members had a book on Melville that was about to be released. The lecture went all right, and I don't recall any specific challenge made to my treatment of Melville. The rest of the examination also went well. After my BA in English in 1939, I had a PhD, twelve years later.

14

A Play with a Purpose and Leaving Home

When we returned to Antofagasta, we brought back a Hammond electronic organ given by our principal supporting church. We unpacked it on the tiled terrace that had been part of the Quinta Casale, the once-elegant restaurant that previously functioned on what became our church property. As we opened the crate, my heart sank. There was a thud of something heavy moving inside the organ's case. The motor had torn loose and was free to smash around inside.

There was no Hammond technician to be called. I had to set about trying to trace contacts and connections, aided by a young friend, a volunteer helper who had some knowledge of things electric. We found that the damage appeared to be less than we had feared. After some reconnections we closed the case, plugged in the cord, and I said to Martha, "Give it a try."

She sat on the organ bench and touched some keys, one by one. They sounded, so she adjusted the Hammond's drawbars, which are its organ stops, spread her hands, and gave it its full voice, playing the Church's *Doxology*. The tiled patio beneath us, the glass-paned front wall of the restaurant's pavilion, the whole space defined by trailing branches of pepper trees, filled and quivered with magnificent sound.

"Praise God, from whom all blessings flow . . ."

"*A Dios, el Padre celestial* . . ."

In either version, English or Spanish, the grand, joyous message of the *Doxology* rolled out that day near the beginning of our second term of service.

We also brought back a tape recorder, something then quite new and correspondingly bulky and heavy. With this we could record our weekly radio program—now a half hour—using the Hammond and making possible such things as two series of short dramatic scripts that I wrote, to be interpreted by members of our congregation. I also enlisted the young Chilean pastor of the nearby Methodist church, who had a fine voice and a distinct flair for drama.

Immediately on our return from furlough, I had set to work with an architect to plan construction on the church property. We proposed a compound of three buildings along the street on the high side of the lot, which sloped toward the lower part of the city. There would be a pastor's residence—what in the Scottish Presbyterian tradition we call the manse—then a student home for girls and, on the corner, the church building. All three would harmonize in white stucco. I wanted roofs of orange-red tile, curved to give a Spanish flavor, but that particular tile proved too expensive. We settled for one of gray cement, still with graceful lines. There would be a wall for privacy and protection, solid below with pickets above, and gates to match.

The manse came first, and work went well—no weather interruptions in a desert climate. The Student Home for Girls had been a project that we first tried in a rented house. In two nitrate mining camps, each of which had a small congregation for which I was responsible, there was only elementary education. For high school, families had to send their sons or daughters down to Antofagasta and find some kind of lodging. For daughters this could be particularly problematic. A student home, duly supervised, could be, for them, a solution, and for us, a group of girls to draw together youth for our nascent church.

The architect and I designed an attractive building—the first floor just a kitchen and a single long room for eating and for study, bright and airy, with one side toward the street and a row of French doors that opened on garden plots and then the fence. The plots had to be small, carefully tended with the city's scant water supply. Upstairs, a corridor ran down one side, with a row of bedrooms, each with two bunk beds, for four girls; and at the end, bathrooms and a private room for the housemother.

It took longer than planned to get this structure up and in use, but we found that the idea worked well. Fees were kept low, and families in the interior were pleased to have the student home available. Martha was able, with some of the resident girls as a nucleus, to form a youth choir.

A Play with a Purpose and Leaving Home

The church construction was the climax. With the clean lines of our buildings, I didn't want any kind of steeple, as I felt that was associated with Catholic architecture. Instead we set, near but separate from the rest of the church structure, a single concrete shaft that had a round window just below the top. The shaft was hollow, with a pulley and cord inside for servicing, to lower the socket of a light behind the window. The frames of all the construction were of reinforced concrete. The whole west coast of South America is part of the earthquake-prone Pacific "Ring of Fire" that arcs from southern Chile, on up Central America, the west coast of North America, across the Bering Strait, then down the east coast of Asia.

We were proud and happy to see our church building completed, bearing in brass letters on its white stucco the name *Iglesia Presbiteriana Cristo Rey*, Christ the King Presbyterian Church.

******

"Pastor! Pastor!"

The man was yelling from the doorway, over the filled pews, to me as I stood in my very new pulpit. He appeared to be a laborer, unkempt, obviously drunk. He started to push forward down the aisle, and a couple of people grabbed and held him. What he knew, and they did not, was that this was a drama, and he was acting a part. It was happening during the Service of Dedication of our new church building.

The service had begun in a conventional way, with the sanctuary packed to overflowing, when abruptly the shouting of the "laborer" erupted. I wrote the script to be that way—realistic and arresting—and the members of our congregation, mostly of the youth group, who were taking parts, entered in enthusiastically. Their youthful nature lent itself well to the emotionally dramatic. Further, I felt that it was important to express dramatically, in this dedicatory service, what we wished and hoped for the new church to become in its community. Now, let me pick up the action as it unfolded on that day.

I called, above the turned heads, "What is it, friend? What do you need?"

"I need to talk to you!"

The people holding the man were ordering him to be quiet.

"Let him come forward," I called out. "Let him speak."

They released the man and, lurching a bit, he started down the central aisle.

"I know I'm drunk," he was saying. "That is the problem. I need help. Can you help me?"

It was not a long aisle. By this time, speaking in broken, anguished phrases, the laborer was near the front. I didn't answer. Instead, a young woman—one of our teenage girls, actually—spoke to him. She had appeared at the back of the chancel, wearing a white surplice, and had come forward quickly.

"I am what you need," she said in a clear, strong voice. "Come up here."

The man came up the three steps at one side of the proscenium and stood facing the girl in white.

"No," he said, "you don't understand. I got drunk. I lost my job. The boss fired me, and now what is my family going to do? I can't stop drinking. It's a curse. I can't stop it."

"I am Purity," the figure in white said. "I am what you need. Here you will find Purity, and you will be helped."

A woman in the congregation began sobbing audibly. I turned toward where she was.

"I don't know you, sister," I said, "but we need you to be quiet, if you can."

"No, I can't," she cried, in a loud wail.

"Then calm yourself," I said. "Come up here and tell us what is troubling you."

The woman left her pew and came up, also, on the raised, open area that was the front of the chancel.

"I'm alone now," she said, still with some sobs in her voice. "He left me. I have no one, no way to live, nothing to live for. I was going to go down to the port and jump off, where it's dark and nobody would see me. I saw light here, and people coming in, and it's new, so I came in."

As she was speaking, a second girl in a white surplice entered from the back of the chancel. "Take heart," she said to the troubled woman, "you are not alone."

"Who are you?" the woman asked.

"I am Compassion. Here you will find compassion—others who also have their troubles, but who will receive and embrace you, and share with you in your need."

The woman walked over to stand beside Compassion, wiping her eyes as she went.

"Well, friends," I said from the pulpit, "now we can continue with the service."

Just then a young man in the front pew stood up.

"Pastor," he said, "these things interest me. I enjoy being a student—a student of life—but it has been getting confusing." He came quickly up the steps to the proscenium.

"My best friend," he continued, "went up to work in the copper mine and came back all convinced about Communism. He says they are the only people who see things as they are; but I wonder. I read this idea and that idea, and my mind turns this way and that."

The third figure to come from the back of the chancel was a young man, also wearing a white surplice. "I am what you are looking for," he said. "I am Truth. Here you can find truth, a secure anchor for your spirit, an eternal rock on which to build your life."

Two children were coming down the center aisle, a girl of seven or eight, with a boy of about four.

"My child, are you looking for someone?" I asked the girl.

"Please, father," she replied, "are you the priest? Someone said we could get help here."

"Perhaps you can," I answered. "We'd like to help you. Come up here and tell us what you need."

As I pointed the way to her, she came up the steps with her brother, who kept gazing around with a small child's wide eyes.

"Our house burned down, and our mom was hurt bad," the child was saying. "They carried her to the hospital, and some neighbors took us in; but the man yelled at my brother and hit him, so we ran away. Do you know anyone here who will help us?"

The girl in white surplice appearing from the back of the chancel was taller than the others, and her voice had a fuller tone.

"I will help you," she said. "I am Love. Love is the heart of our faith here, God's love. In Jesus Christ, God loves you, and we will love you, too."

She put her arms around the children, and I spoke from the pulpit:

"Friends, we invite you to join us here this evening to dedicate this new sanctuary to the worship and service of God. These brothers and sisters of our congregation, taking their various parts, have declared what it is that, by God's grace, we wish this church—as every church of God—to be."

There were a few more words, some hymns and prayers as that memorable service drew to a close.

Change was in the air. In New York, the venerable Presbyterian Board of Foreign Missions was contemplating reorganization, even to changing its name. The pattern of maintaining foreign missions that were composed only of missionaries from the United States, working under the direction of the New York board, should be relegated to the past. Instead, the administrative body of the Presbyterian Church in each of those countries should assume full responsibility for institutions and whatever other projects the mission had been administering. Thus, funds and support from the mission board in the United States would pass directly to the church administrative body of that country—which also might make requests directly to the board.

Further, the board's missionaries would now be called fraternal workers. They would serve under the direction and responsibility of the national church's governing body. In addition, the governing body could request the appointment of more workers, according to its perception of needs and opportunities.

These were far-reaching changes, and in most regions they would be accomplished progressively. In Chile, we received a visit by a top-level staff delegation from New York. Some of us were enthusiastic about a plan for radical restructuring. Another young missionary, who was principal of the school in Valparaíso, joined me in pushing for it. The Chile mission, as an administrative body, should be dissolved, and its members should be called "fraternal workers," the name that was beginning to be used elsewhere.

More than that, as the Chilean Presbyterians took over full responsibility, we "fraternal workers" would entirely be withdrawn. There were some who were approaching retirement. As they left, they would not be replaced. The rest of us would complete our current terms of service, and when we left on furlough, we would not expect to return. After an interval, the Presbytery of Chile might ask New York for a fraternal worker with special preparation to help with a particular project; but that would be on specific terms and for a limited time. Thus, at the end of the reform, there would be no foreign missionaries deployed under the authority of New York. Any foreign "fraternal workers" would be at the invitation and under the authority of the national church.

It was an extraordinary experience, especially for members who had spent most of their active years in the country, when the Chile mission met

A Play with a Purpose and Leaving Home

to talk about the plan and then to vote, in solemn session, to request the board in New York that the mission be dissolved.

Martha and I had about three years left before the end of our second term. This meant that we would work even harder to help our Antofagasta congregation reach a point of self-sufficiency. There had to be church officers, who are lay leaders mature enough to care for all church business and to guide the developing life of the congregation. And this meant that, above all, the combined giving of the congregation must support a budget that could include funds to call and to pay the salary of a Chilean pastor.

This would mean, for the new church, a phase of maturity. It would also be, for Martha and me in Antofagasta, the fulfillment of the saying that we were there "to work ourselves out of a job."

*****

"Daddy, I want to go with you."

That was María, our household helper. She had adopted from the children a custom of calling me "Daddy" and Martha "Mama" (although they generally used "Mom"), even though Martha was her senior by only eight years. María had been with us since our return to Antofagasta for our second term. She had grown close to the children, who by this time were four: Donna, Sylvia, Tommy, and Marilyn. The "you" María wanted to leave with was all of us. She used the Spanish plural pronoun for "you."

"But, María, you know that we are not coming back."

"Yes, I know," she answered, "but I want to go."

"You would be leaving your parents, your family, your homeland. It's a long journey, and I wouldn't be able to send you back."

"I know, I know," she said. "Now this is my family, and I want to go."

Martha and I talked it over. Certainly, María would be a help. Martha was pregnant again, and I would be busy with my new position. The New York Board had invited me to replace the liaison person for the Caribbean Area, who was leaving, and they wanted me to start immediately on our return to the United States. That would mean a lot of travel, linking our missions and churches in Venezuela, Colombia, Guatemala, and Mexico. We all loved María, and her help would be very timely, but we'd also be taking on a sobering responsibility.

In the end, we said yes, and I secured a ticket for María. She would share a cabin with our older girls, on the Grace Line ship on which we had passage to New York.

That final morning, we stood at the ship's rail, looking down into the faces of our friends—our sisters and brothers at Christ the King, with whom we had formed a closed bond across the years that were now ending. María's family was there, too.

The hugs and kisses and affectionate words ended, as the "all ashore" had sounded. Now, after long delay, the gangway was being cranked up; hawsers were cast off, and a crack of dark water was showing between the ship's hull and the dock. Our children were brimming with excitement. Donna was old enough to stand by herself; but María had Sylvia and Tommy, one with each hand, while Martha held onto little Marilyn. I called some last words down, cut short as the captain gave our ship's horn a blast.

The ship swung slowly around, then out, making the breakwater's miniature lighthouse slip by. We moved to an aft rail to watch as the expanding water spread between us and the city, the hills, the desert land that we had made to be our family's home.

How would it be for María? When we agreed to her travel, we could only hope for the best. In fact, she was with our family in the United States for a year. After that, we all moved to Mexico City, as a base for my position and travel. There, María met, fell in love with, and married a university graduate from Yucatán. In 1960, I left mission work and our family moved to Texas. María and her husband made their home in Yucatán. Sadly, he died rather young; but she has lived out many years in Mérida with her two daughters, and later their children.

By the generosity of a relative in Chile, María did see Antofagasta again, on a visit, making the long flight down and back. Martha and I were able to visit María twice over the years, and have stayed in close touch with the family. She is now in her late eighties, with health problems, but continues in her home, with care and love from her daughters and grandchildren.

15

Caribbean Travel and A Front-Lawn Wedding

ARRIVING IN NEW YORK, our family had the use of a fourth-floor apartment in upper Manhattan for half a year. It was still winter, a radical change from balmy January in northern Chile's Southern Hemisphere climate. Martha arranged for Donna and Sylvia to be enrolled at St. Hilda's, an Episcopal school a couple of blocks away. Going back and forth, they had to cope with a cold wind off the Hudson River that funneled up a cross street. All of this was new—being in the great city, being in school, and, for María, being in the United States (even though there was plenty of Spanish on signs and in street talk around us).

My new assignment meant that I had no break. My predecessor, Dick Baird, was anxious to turn over the job, while he also wanted to help me get a good start. Like me, he was a son of Korea missionaries, although of a generation earlier than mine. Dick had been sent back to Korea in his own right; but then World War II came, and he was re-assigned to Latin America. Now it was arranged by the board that he should guide me on a three-week tour of the Caribbean Area, introducing me to people and to situations I should be acquainted with.

Those were three long weeks. The family adjustment to city life in New York fell mostly on Martha, which was hard for her; and my initiation to an assignment that would mean much travel, away from home, was not easy for me. Dick was a good companion, though, and very helpful. I needed to get the feel of being a liaison person, linked to the church and leadership of the four countries on my beat—Venezuela, Colombia, Guatemala, and Mexico—while also representing the mission board in New York. I had an advantage over Dick, with the years in Chile behind me and the fluency in language and custom that these had given me.

Of our travels together, one memorable location was up the Sinu River Valley in tropical Colombia. Dick and his wife had worked there, in a rural community, for several years, before he was given the Caribbean Area assignment. He told me how he got used to the steaming heat, night and day, with almost no seasonal variation. Why pick such a place? Because the Presbyterian Church had taken root there. Rural Colombia tends to be strongly, even fanatically Roman Catholic; but the independent-minded country folk far up this river valley had staunchly embraced Protestant faith and worship. We rode up the broad valley for half a day in a truck that at times seemed to be following nothing more than a dim track across wide pastures, pausing at fences while a boy jumped down to open a gate, then close it behind us.

That evening I spoke to the church people, gathered by lantern light. They were warmly responsive. I had to think of First Century clusters of Christian believers—the simple sincerity of their conviction drawn from the Apostle Paul, their mentor, who is also very much my spiritual mentor. Dick told me how content he had been, living and working there; how he had thought that, as he put it, he would leave his bones there in the Sinu River Valley.

That was Dick Baird, accepting life as it was given. In one airport he pointed out a No Smoking sign, *No fume.*

"See?" he commented, humorously. "Don't get impatient and upset; the sign says, 'Don't fume!'"

The church people gave me a wide-brimmed straw hat, soft and resilient, woven from a fine grass that grows there. I have it, yet, on a closet shelf, to remember that steaming valley and its people.

Back in New York, it was a heady time. Across the nation, church attendance was up and church finances strong. At the same time, as I've indicated, important changes were taking place abroad: foreign missions being dissolved and missionaries becoming fraternal workers, directed by and serving under the church agencies of the country where they worked. In keeping with all of this, the Board of Foreign Missions of the Presbyterian Church in the U.S.A. was getting a new name. It would now be the Commission on Ecumenical Mission and Relations, or COEMAR (KOH-mahr).

Caribbean Travel and a Front-Lawn Wedding

From New York, COEMAR General Secretary Charles T. Leber sent out a call to the headquarters of all of the churches, worldwide, which were related with the Presbyterian Church U.S.A. Would each one send a representative to a conference on mission strategy and needs, to be held at Lake Mohonk in central New York State? Martha and I were to be there, along with other COEMAR personnel. This would be my first such event in my new capacity, and an exciting one.

Early in the conference, as a sort of get-acquainted icebreaker, there was an informal evening program for which each regional delegation would put on some kind of act to make itself better known. The Latin American representatives—from Cuba, Mexico, Colombia, Guatemala, Venezuela, and Chile—huddled with Martha and me. What could they do? They decided to sing something and found that they all knew *Las Mañanitas*, a popular love song. We didn't know it.

"How does it go?" Martha asked. "Sing it for me."

One of them started out, while Martha listened, sitting at a piano. As the song went along, she began to join in softly with some chords. Soon she had it, and finished, along with the singer, as if she knew the song as well as he did. The group was amazed and delighted, and Martha definitely was "in."

There was another memorable moment that same evening. While the Latin American group was still on the improvised stage after their song, someone asked a question about the revolutionary movement in Cuba, which seemed in process of establishing itself. How did they, as Protestant Christians, feel about this? After some words among themselves, these delegates, unanimously, raised their hands high, calling out fervently, "*Con Fidel hasta la muerte!*" With Fidel (Castro), to the death! Cuban Communism then, and in the future, accepted Protestant churches and their causes.

The large hotel at Lake Mohonk, where we were all lodged, was right on the water. One afternoon I found a one-person rowboat. There were still some vestiges of ice at the water's edges, but it was bracing, and very refreshing, to pull at the oars and get a different sense of the setting and our being there.

After a half year in New York City, we moved to Princeton, to one of the now-familiar Payne Hall apartments. With María, we were a family of seven: three adults and four children, with a fifth child now on the way. The two-bedroom/one-bath apartment made for a very tight fit, even though we added a bed at one side in the dining room and made other accommodations. In Princeton María found a congenial group of Latin American friends, while we also encouraged her to keep working at English. For the new baby's arrival, Martha arranged to go back to the hospital in Riverside, New Jersey, where Tom had been born on our previous furlough. María was closely involved in all of this; so, the newest addition, Alan, was special to her, and he always continued to be. She liked to call him *Cielito*, Little Heaven.

*****

For my work I needed to be back in a Latin American setting and nearer to my area. After our half year in Princeton, the plan was to move to Mexico City. We had a well-used seven-passenger station wagon, supplied by COEMAR, and that would do well for our journey. Tourist visas were easily secured. We knew that in Mexico obtaining a long-term residence permit was a quite different matter; but that could wait.

Crossing the border at Laredo, Texas, it was exciting for the family to be in Mexico! The countryside was dry like Texas; but this was different from northern Chile, which only our older three children could at all remember. We were going to learn that the greater difference is in the Mexican cultural orientation. As we were entering the environs of Mexico City, we were confronted by a large and striking proof of that difference. In the center of a traffic circle where major highways meet, a monument had been raised. It was—and is—a copy in design and shape of a Mayan stone pyramid. At the base, where flights of steps ascend, we saw statues: heroic male and female figures in stone, carved massively with Aztec and Mayan features. The monument, so strongly indigenous, is named *Monumento a la Raza*, Monument to the Race.

Mexico City was far less populated then, in the late 1950s, than the smothering metropolis that it has become. We rented a pleasant, Spanish-style country house with a generous, gated yard, on one edge of the city in a district known, intriguingly, as *Desierto de Los Leones* (Desert of the Lions). We promptly began negotiations for a legal stay in the country. Although Mexico was welcoming to tourists, a valuable source of revenue, as long-term residents, foreigners were regarded as potentially taking jobs that Mexicans should have. Since I needed to travel, with freedom to move in and out of the country, I would have to remain a tourist, periodically renewing my tourist visa.

Caribbean Travel and a Front-Lawn Wedding

For Martha, the avenue was to establish her as a *rentista*, a person receiving an independent income from abroad. After months of negotiation, this required that she should leave the country, have her passport stamped with a permanent visa, and then return—the whole procedure dependent on the promptitude and good will of the consulate at the border. This meant that the children must go with her, as they were on her passport.

We left María to care for the house and again piled into the station wagon for a reverse trip to Laredo, finding a tourist hostelry there on a pond, for splashing and keeping cool. The procedure took several days, as expected. When Martha was questioned by the border official I, the tourist, stayed out of sight, wanting to avoid raising any complications.

The official looked at the children surrounding Martha and asked, in all seriousness, "Miss, are you married?"

In the course of our three years in Mexico City, I made frequent trips out and back into the country on my intermittently renewed tourist visa. I was often uneasy, wondering when my "tourist" status might be challenged and I might be shut out, with my family inside.

Those were transition years. In my liaison position as Commission Representative, mediating between COEMAR, in New York, and the missions and national church bodies in the four countries on my Caribbean circuit, I focused on helping dissolve the missions in three of them—Venezuela, Colombia, and Guatemala. We followed the pattern we had used in Chile. This brought me in close association with leaders of the national churches, a development that could cut two ways.

It was gratifying and fulfilling when, after a discussion with a group of Guatemalan leaders, one of them said to me, "You are one of us."

On the other hand, I confronted a different response when a similar Guatemalan group was pressing for a series of requests for funds from New York. The amount seemed to me to be out of balance with what the Guatemalans themselves should be doing. In the heat of the discussion, I said, "You don't want to be little nephews of Uncle Sam."

That remark hit the fan! The discussion stopped, and I was told later, indirectly, that I must apologize. I did; although I had spoken out of concern that the national churches—in this case the Guatemalan—should stand on their own feet. I recognized that I had touched a nerve.

In Mexico City we rounded out our family. Martha went through a final pregnancy, and in the British American Hospital gave birth to our sixth child, curly-headed Larry (Lawrence Paul). Of course, he wasn't curly-headed yet; but by the time he was getting around, then learning to walk, his head was a mass of blond-gold ringlets. He was a happy child, with plenty of siblings for companionship.

It was while Larry was still an infant, though, that word came to us from Martha's family in New Jersey. Her father was very ill. She needed to go immediately to see him, while he was still alive.

Of course, she would go; but what about baby Larry? She was breastfeeding him. We would have to get him included on her passport, so that she could take him out of the country and bring him back in. Inquiry at the United States Consulate laid out a bureaucratic process requiring too many days; but there was a speedier solution. Mexican authorities would issue to Larry, this tiny, native-born citizen, his own Mexican passport, complete with his three-or-four-month-old photograph. So equipped, he made the flights up and back in his mother's arms. We were all relieved, and Martha saw her father before he died, which was several months later.

María was not much involved, though. She had met a university student from the Yucatán Peninsula who was finishing his studies, as I mentioned in the previous chapter, and rather soon we learned that they were in love. Our rented house, with its graceful Spanish lines, had a broad, sloping lawn that was level enough, near the house, to serve as the site for a charming, wedding. Donna and Sylvia were bridesmaids and Marilyn, flower girl; all wore dresses that Martha made. She played the little organ, and I proudly officiated. María's new husband, Waldemaro Canto, soon secured a government job as a supervisor of stored agricultural produce in Yucatán. We were happy to see how happy *she* was, and how well situated.

*****

During our stay in Mexico, my parents came from New York City to visit us. Dad was retired and had a project: a book about his missionary experience and the unfolding of the medical work in Taegu at both the general and leprosy hospitals. He had collected letters and reports, and he and Mother had a wealth of anecdotes and remembered experiences. Their idea was that I should take such time as my home and work duties might allow, to talk with them and to begin to write the book that Dad envisioned. On our rental property there was a very small house in a grove, quite separate from the main house. They could live there for several months, while we had a try at Dad's project.

Caribbean Travel and A Front-Lawn Wedding

I was eager to do my part, and we gave it an earnest try. Time was hard to come by, but I did what I could. The Presbyterian Mexico mission had a rest house some miles from the city, on a deep, clear lake formed by a long-extinct volcano. I took some time off work and we went down to the rest house for a week or so—just Mother, Dad, and I—to work as intensively as we could.

In the end, months after my parents' return to New York, we had enough sketched out for Dad to show to a friend in the New York office who worked in promotion and who made efforts to find a publisher. I was in New York City on a business trip when this friend arranged a meeting with a representative of one of the publishing houses. The man was friendly and seemed interested, but nothing came of it. For my part, I had too much else on my plate at that time to give the rejection much thought.

Happily, that was not end of the story or of Dad's literary ambition and effort: in 2016, almost sixty years later, I completed rewriting and expanding the manuscript, which was published that year as *By Scalpel and Cross: A Missionary Doctor in Old Korea*.

16

A Gospel Parable and a Department to Chair

WHEN I HAD BEEN in my Caribbean Area post for four years, COEMAR made some changes and eliminated the post. I could have applied for something else; but Martha and I decided that our service in Latin America and in the world mission cause was finishing. We were being led by the Spirit in a new direction.

My longtime friend John Jansen, a classmate and fellow English major at Princeton twenty-one years earlier, had also entered the Presbyterian ministry and had gone on to become a professor of New Testament studies. John was now on the faculty of the Presbyterian Theological Seminary in Austin, Texas, and he knew of my situation.

John also knew that in Austin there was going to be a vacancy in the Presbyterian Bible Chair at the University of Texas. These Bible chairs were a curiously hybrid phenomenon. Located in the Bible Belt, the university felt pressure to offer elective courses in biblical studies, such as "The Life and Teachings of Jesus." But for a state university to do so would appear to violate the constitutional separation of church and state. The compromise was the creation of Bible chairs independently supported by various religious denominations, which paid their instructors and provided facilities off-campus, so that no public funds were used. The university, for its part, awarded elective credit for such courses, exercising a loose oversight of the instructors, while not giving them faculty status. The Presbyterian Bible

Chair was supported through Austin Presbyterian Theological Seminary, where John helped secure my appointment.

This was a new life for us. The seminary gave us the use of a house that it owned—large and rambling, on a weedy, half-acre lot near the seminary's campus. The burden of our family's adjustment, returning to an English-speaking world, as well as the quite special, Hispanic-tinctured world of central Texas, again rested mostly on Martha. She got five of our six children enrolled in school, ranging from pre-K to eighth grade, while adjusting herself to shopping, cooking, and keeping house, with the conveniences and shortcuts of American urban life in 1960, but without the assistance of our cheerful Mexican household help.

Our children had their own adjustments to make, particularly the older three. In parenting, Martha and I had made it a basic rule to recognize and respect the personhood of each child, even the youngest. Sylvia, our second child, had put that to the test from when she was very small. She was definitely, sometimes emphatically, her own person. At the same time, she was sensitive and caring, particularly toward animals.

When we moved to Austin, Sylvia was ten. Sometime in that first or second year she persuaded us to let her adopt a small cat from a shelter. Pawsie, so named by her for distinctive forepaw markings, turned out to be a male. He would roam at night, coming running to her when she went out to call him in the morning. His male nature showed quite often in evidence of nocturnal catfights.

It was perhaps inevitable that one morning Pawsie barely made it home, severely wounded. Martha let Sylvia set up a cat care center on top of the clothes dryer in the screened area by the back door. There, Sylvia tended Pawsie's wounds until he died. She found a shoe box, lined it carefully with some pieces of cloth and laid in it the small body. Her grief was heartbreaking.

"We will bury Pawsie," I said to her, "just you and I."

Avoiding the curious attention of any other family members, I got a spade and we selected a spot in the side, weedy lot where our seminary house stood. I dug a sufficient hole; we set in the box, and then I spoke a prayer. For me, it was altogether appropriate. We weren't play-acting a human funeral. We were giving thanks for one of God's creatures, for its small life that had given us meaning. Gently we filled in the earth and pressed it firm.

*****

I had a sequestered study on one side of the house, with space for the carved, Chilean-oak desk and bookcases that were still with us after our several moves. What I faced professionally was daunting. My seminary studies had included overviews of the complex, varied writings in the Bible, and I had read and preached from the biblical texts in both English and Spanish across some twenty years. This, however, was different. My new situation was encapsulated in an informal gathering arranged to introduce me to a group of students at Austin Seminary. They were interested in my views on Bible teaching and interpretation.

"What about Bultmann?" one of them asked.

The reference was to the German New Testament scholar Rudolf Bultmann. His views recorded in *Jesus and the Word* and other influential writings of that time were revolutionizing, especially for many young students such as these. I had heard Bultmann's name spoken but knew nothing of him at first hand, so my reply to the question had to be hedging and non-committal.

This kind of challenge in biblical scholarship was new to me. It was unnerving at times but also wonderfully exhilarating. I would be offering, as occupant of the Presbyterian Bible Chair, a course on "The Life and Teachings of Jesus." This meant getting quickly into contemporary scholarship and discussion on the New Testament Gospels. As I did so, I found myself questioning and rethinking attitudes and assumptions that I had carried with me since childhood.

This gave me a new freedom and challenge. I wasn't abandoning faith; but along with discoveries and fresh ways of thinking, I was entering on a vivid awareness of the historical world of the Gospels, and of Jesus himself in that setting, as well as the relevance of his message for our time.

Among the remembered sayings of Jesus, one parable, recorded in Luke's Gospel, chapter 16, verses 1–13, intrigued me. Known as the Parable of the Unjust Steward (or Dishonest Manager, in the *New Revised Standard Version*), it tells a story of a steward, turned out on the street by his master, who connives with the master's debtors to rewrite their debts, assuring for himself that they will take him in when he is destitute. The master, when he learns this, congratulates the steward for his devious cleverness for, as Jesus says, "the children of this age are more shrewd in dealing with their own generation than are the children of light." What is the point of the parable? In Luke's text, Jesus goes on to say to his followers:

A Gospel Parable and a Department to Chair

"And I tell you, make friends for yourselves by means of dishonest wealth, so that when it is gone, they may welcome you into the eternal homes" (Luke 16:9 NRSV).

The message is surprising. And the parable itself, as remembered and passed along, to be set down by Luke some fifty or sixty years later—how probable does it seem, as something Jesus would have related? After I had been teaching in Austin for two years, I had confidence to investigate and research the parable. I had become acquainted with the internationally recognized Society of Biblical Literature and its quarterly publication, the *Journal of Biblical Literature*. The method of scholarly investigation that I used was what I had learned during graduate study and dissertation writing at Princeton University.

Through the summer months and into the fall of 1962, I worked on the Unjust Steward, researching everything I could find on how this seemingly contradictory teaching of Jesus had been interpreted by scholars from as far back as John Calvin himself. And as I studied it, what came through to me, as one keenly interested in the use of language, was that the thrust of Jesus' startling saying, as it was remembered, was heavily ironic. Curiously, none of the interpreters I found, whether early or contemporary, read it that way.

I had the makings of an article that could genuinely be a scholarly contribution. It needed to be written as carefully and logically as possible, with meticulous attention to footnotes and academic details; careful, too, the typing of the text, which I did myself (no convenience in that era of electronic preparation and transmission). My article was titled, "The Riddle of the Unjust Steward: Is Irony the Key?" I sent it off that fall, with great respect and scant expectation, to the Editor of the *Journal of Biblical Literature*.

Imagine my amazement, my rush of utter gratification, when the Spring 1963 issue of the *Journal*, Volume LXXXII, Part 1, came out and mine was the second article of eight listed on the front cover (as they did it then)! I have a copy alongside me as I write this, fifty-five years later. My original, well-thumbed copy was lost along the way; but with the marvel of the electronic age, my daughter found it on line and presented me with this pristine copy.

*****

Those were the early 1960s, an acute phase of the civil rights struggle in America's South. We heard about it in Texas but were not swept into it. Then came 1964, the Freedom Summer, and stark headlines. Three young "freedom" workers—Cheney, Schwerner, and Goodman, the first, an African American born there, the second and third white activists from the North—were murdered in Mississippi.

A call went out for clergy of any faith to go to Mississippi, to volunteer for a week just to accompany the teams of young men and women who were going from door to door, encouraging black Mississippians to register to vote. The clergies' presence, it was felt, would serve as a deterrent to violence.

I volunteered. This was called the Hattiesburg Ministers Project. When I arrived at the staging area (I don't remember just where that was) I found myself in an intensive orientation session that included vivid roleplay to prepare volunteers for dangerous situations into which we might be thrust. For example, how to respond if in a car stopped by a white sheriff. All provocations, no matter how belligerent, had to be warded off rather than confronted.

The orientation ended with all participants forming a circle. We crossed arms in the way later to become so familiar and were led in singing "We Shall Overcome." I had not heard it sung and found it profoundly moving. The evening was growing late when we broke up. Those of us in the Ministers' Project were taken to a firehouse in the heart of Hattiesburg's black community, where we would be housed.

For the next, memorable week, I moved around the city and its environs, wherever I was sent, usually accompanying a team of young voter-registration volunteers. One day, however, because of my association with the University of Texas, I was put on campus at the University of Southern Mississippi, which is in Hattiesburg. I was just to mingle and converse with students or faculty, helping to establish in a friendly way our supportive purpose in being there. The students—all white, of course—who I was able to engage in conversation were generally polite and sometimes receptive, as were some junior faculty. I did encounter an older faculty member who was less cordial, and later was told by a guard that one of the deans said I should report to him.

When I promptly did so, the dean confronted me, immediately hostile. I tried to assure him that I was not there to stir up any kind of encounter, but he was stern and brief. I had not been invited by the university, was

A Gospel Parable and a Department to Chair

persona non grata, should be off the campus within twenty minutes and should stay off, or he would instruct security to put me off. So ended my assignment on the campus of the University of Southern Mississippi.

On Sunday morning a couple of us went to a Presbyterian church in a suburban area. We were greeted cordially enough, but when we identified ourselves as pleasantly as we could, we were asked to wait, while the pastor was consulted. Perhaps he didn't wish to have a face-to-face confrontation. The elder we had spoken with came back to say to us,

"Please leave now. You aren't welcome here."

There was a younger member of the university faculty who was openly sympathetic with our cause. One evening I was with several others, including young Northern volunteers, who were gathered in his home. Abruptly, he interrupted a conversation, asking a young black woman to move to a seat at one side of the room. It was a warm night. The front door was open, and he had realized that from the shrubbery outside, there was a clear shot through that doorway to where she had been sitting.

The transforming part of my week in Hattiesburg was how radically, although not consciously, I found some of my feelings change. The sight of any white person in uniform made me uncomfortable, and the police were downright intimidating. Conversely, when I was back at our firehouse in the black community, I felt safe and at ease. When my volunteering stint was up and our northbound bus reached the state line, the sign stating that we were leaving Mississippi gave me a curious, momentary surge of relief deep inside.

*****

David Stitt, President of Austin Seminary, collaborated with me in arranging for the Methodist and Disciples of Christ student centers to join with us in creating a United Bible Chair. We pooled our resources and were able to offer a more effective program. I served as director of the new enterprise, and all went well for two years. Then the Methodists announced that they were withdrawing; which collapsed our three-legged stool. David said that the seminary budget could not afford a return to a fulltime Presbyterian Bible Chair instructor. So, I was again out of a job.

One evening during that final spring, David and Jane Stitt came to visit Martha and me. Martha had for some time been Director of Music at the large University Presbyterian Church, where for the first time in her career, she had a good choir and a superb organist to work with. She had recently prepared, directed, and produced a performance of Bach's wonderful *St. Matthew Passion*, in which Jane Stitt, who had a pleasing voice, sang one of the solo parts. David and Jane, along with all of the friends at University Presbyterian, wanted very much to keep Martha in Austin.

David had an offer for me. The seminary would be needing a librarian. I had the academic background for the position, and they would arrange for me to pick up some technical instruction in order to be fully qualified. The librarian job would be my entire responsibility; I would not do any teaching.

I asked a question or two to make sure that I had a precise picture of the offer. Then I said, "Thank you, David. I appreciate, very much, your kind interest in my situation and the offer of a position on the seminary staff; but I don't see it as a possible direction I might take."

There wasn't much more to be said. For me, being a librarian, with no chance to teach, would be a dead end. We all continued as friends; although David remarked later that I might at least have said I'd need to think it over for a day or two.

Soon after that, a way forward opened up for us. Stillman College, in Tuscaloosa, Alabama, needed someone to chair its Department of English. Located in the same city as the University of Alabama, Stillman was a historically black college of Presbyterian affiliation. From the standpoint of racial integration, it was an uneasy time. Tuscaloosa did not have the feel of the Deep South I had experienced in Hattiesburg, but there was unrest; after all, it was surrounded by Deep South Alabama. In my department I had several young instructors from Northern graduate schools who had applied to teach at Stillman because of their support of the civil rights cause.

I recall one evening when a crowd of students surrounded the home of the Dean of the College, wanting him to accede to some demand they were making. A couple of my instructors were in the thick of it. Martha, who was in the Department of Music, and I were careful to remain uninvolved in such conflicts, supportive of the college authorities while also wanting to understand our students and their world. The dean, who was African-American, told me how, at a recent meeting of educators that was held in a downtown hotel, he had to use the freight elevator. That was still his world in the mid-1960s.

A response of Stillman College to the changing time was that it was installing the first black president in its history. I was also wishing to see a senior black member of the English Department move into my position, and

A Gospel Parable and a Department to Chair

Martha was experiencing a similar situation in the music department. She and I were feeling that we should move on to make space for these changes. Our two years in Tuscaloosa had been both instructive and enjoyable. Just at that juncture came an invitation to me to try something different.

I got a telephone call from a staff member of the Presbyterian Board of Christian Education, which then had its offices in the historic Witherspoon Building in downtown Philadelphia. He was on a tour through several southern states. Could Martha and I meet him to talk about something that might interest us? We drove to the place he suggested, and over a couple of hours he enthusiastically laid before us an attractive opportunity.

The board in Philadelphia, in its Continuing Education Division, was creating a new position. Larger Presbyterian churches around the country had on their staffs a fulltime person employed to carry forward the church's program of Christian education—via Sunday School, weekday released-time classes, adult study groups, and the like. The board wanted to appoint a Secretary of Continuing Education for Professional Church Educators. Would I be interested?

Of course, I was interested—shall I say nervously intrigued? Could I qualify? Martha went with me to the interview, and our interviewer knew about my training and experience, and was confident that I did qualify, pointing out that this was a new position. I would establish my own goals and make my way toward them.

When that interview ended, we were committed. Martha, even more than I, felt drawn back to the Northeast, to the part of the country that was native to her. I had family ties to the Northeast, as well, and that was where I had sunk my intellectual roots.

17

A Last Supper and a Madonna by Raphael

WE WERE MAKING OUR last whole-family move—all eight of us. Our eldest, Donna, had had two years of college, one each at the Universities of Texas and Alabama; and Sylvia had just graduated from high school. We decided to settle in Cherry Hill, New Jersey, where we could afford an adequate house, where schools were good, and from which I had an easy commute to my office in Philadelphia. Martha's reputation seemed to have preceded her. Before we started on our journey back to the Northeast, she had a call from the organizing pastor of the new, rapidly growing Trinity Presbyterian Church in Cherry Hill. He was offering her the position of organist and director of music.

My new job called for new skills, some of which did not come easily to me. The primary method for enhancing the abilities of people engaged professionally in religious education was to bring them together regionally in small groups for an intensive three-or-four-day seminar. My role was to arrange these, to plan programs and secure leadership, including myself, and to maintain the correspondence in a time of no email and, certainly, no smartphones. Fortunately, in my office, I had a patient and helpful secretary.

In that era, our seminars had an innovative side. Sensitivity training was in vogue. Participants might engage, blindfolded, in "trust walks," or try out other techniques and devices to enhance interpersonal skills and increase awareness, acceptance and dependence on one another. The idea was to give them something to carry back to their places and people of service. As for me, I was glad to participate in events that more experienced staff of our Philadelphia offices put on, and to learn all that I could. At the same time, as I got more into this work, I was finding some greater freedom of expression, some easing, perhaps, of the tightness of my natural introversion.

I had been only a few months in my position on the staff of the Board of Christian Education when word went around that a "Langner Event" was being planned. This turned out to involve some twelve to fifteen of us, with particular focus on new staff members. We flew to New Mexico, then went overland to Ghost Ranch, a Presbyterian conference center in a somewhat isolated, beautiful setting among rocky cliffs and clefts in the southern part of the state. The event was entirely in the hands of Dr. Langner, himself, a psychiatrist who as I recall was from Phoenix. He conducted group sessions, while he and his assistant also put those of us who were new through some psychological tests on the side.

In my case, he called me in, reviewing the test results. "This looks more like a diploma than a set of recommendations," he said. "Everything seems to be fine."

I have one vivid recollection from the Langner Event. The doctor made effective use of role-playing and simple, improvised psycho-drama. Learning some details of each person's life, he would zero in on a situation that he thought might be used to bring out some need. He would set up a scene, using that person and one or two others to play roles in acting it out.

When it was my turn, he had picked up a mention, in my early life's story, of how I was sent away from home to boarding school when I was only ten. Dr. Langner had me talk about that, trying to get at it in different ways, but without success. Then he singled out two other participants to be my parents and said, "Now, this is your last supper." We were to sit at a table and talk, as if I were leaving the next morning for boarding-school.

Still, it wasn't working. I tried to imagine the scene and say what I might have said; but it remained flat.

"All right," Dr. Langner said, "now it's bedtime." He had me lie on a sofa, and the participant who was my "mother" came and sat on the edge to say goodnight, with reassuring words.

Suddenly, it took hold. I could hear my own voice trying to answer and breaking down in a sobbing cry that seemed to pour out from far away, from a child at a long-distant time. My "mother" put her arm around me, and Dr. Langner called a halt. He was always careful not to push beyond any limits; but I can still hear, in my mind, that lonely, desolate, unbodied cry. How deep such an unexpected well of feeling can be!

The Langner Event ended, and we returned to Philadelphia—I, with a memory still vivid after these five decades.

My work involved travel, being away for events here and there, across the country. During those times Martha carried the full weight of home and family responsibility as she had done when I was traveling in the Caribbean area. A benefit of a large family, though, was that our six children always did much to help each other, caring for and about one another, and passing along their learning of their experiences.

Meanwhile, my parents had made their own decisive move. In Duarte, a suburb of Los Angeles, a Chinese Christian businessman had made the initial gift to establish a community for retired Presbyterian missionaries. Westminster Gardens, as it was named, offered independent cottages as well as continuing care facilities, according to its residents' needs. Mother and Dad left the Manhattan apartment where they had lived for some years and moved west to Westminster Gardens.

A benefit of the travel that my job required was that occasionally I could arrange a stopover there for a visit. My parents had a pleasant cottage and things went well for a time. Then Dad began to show signs of dementia. Quite alarming was an incident that occurred when Mother was awakened from a nap by his trying to bind a belt around her ankles. He had some notion that she wanted to go away with another man. Such fantasies seemed to haunt him—to the point that she spoke with the supervisor of the Gardens, who helped to arrange, diplomatically, for her and Dad to give up their cottage and move to a building where they had a two-room apartment, with principal meals in a common dining room. On one occasion, I visited them there and, with my irregular hours of air travel, was catching a nap in the bedroom. Dad came in and stood quite a while, just looking at me. He knew who I was, and yet seemed unsure, doubtful about this man in their bedroom.

My opportunities for contact were infrequent. By the next one, Dad's condition had deteriorated, and he had been moved to the Gardens' nursing care facility. I visited him there at lunch time, as he sat with a retired missionary educator who had worked, I think, in China. The conversation was cordial, but confined to fragments, at best.

In due time I had a call from Mother: Dad had died. It came as I was leaving home on a major assignment. She assured me that at Westminster

Gardens everything would be taken care of. There would be an intimate service for residents and friends, and interment, after cremation, in a plot they had bought in the nearby cemetery.

Archie, my brother, was in India on his missionary assignment. Our sister, Elsie, in Nashville, was flying out to California the next day, in time for the memorial service.

I told Mother that I would come for a good visit as soon as my continuing-education event, which was in San Francisco, was finished. I thought to myself that Elsie would give her support for a day or two; then, when a let-down might come, I would be there.

In effect, it seemed to work out well. On my visits I would always rent a car, usually a Volkswagen "Beetle," at an economy agency a couple of blocks from the airport terminal. Now I took Mother out to do an errand and then try out, for dinner, a Mexican restaurant that I had noticed. She seemed to enjoy that, and I had *huevos rancheros*, which I certainly enjoyed. She was going to miss Dad, even though, as she said, he had no longer been himself when she visited him daily in the nursing center.

*****

In March of 1971, Martha and I decided on an adventure. Our children were growing up. Donna, twenty-three, had graduated from the University of Kansas and was working in Kansas City. Sylvia was about to graduate from Wellesley in Boston, and Tom, finishing a second year at the University of Tennessee, was leaning toward transferring to American University in Washington. They would soon be taking their various roads in life. Even the younger ones were maturing: Marilyn and Alan in high school; and Larry, our youngest, about to turn thirteen. We would take the month of August, all eight of us, to travel together in Europe.

It would be done economically. We would cross the Atlantic on Icelandic Airlines. Since we needed a new car, I would arrange with the Renault agent in New Jersey to have a Renault wagon delivered in Paris, for all eight of us to squeeze in with our suitcases tied to a roof rack. At the end of our adventure, the car would be loaded on a ship and we would claim it in New Jersey's Port Elizabeth and keep it Stateside. My salary wasn't large, and Martha's, as a church musician, was even smaller. For the first time in my life, I borrowed money, bought a bundle of traveler's cheques, and we booked our flight.

In Paris, where we had planned to spend two or three days, our stay at our economy hotel extended into a second week. The pre-ordered Renault had not been delivered. Monsieur Dreyfus, the amiable agent, kept assuring us that it must be on the next barge coming down the Seine. For our part, we could only wait, sightseeing the City of Light in detail, while reducing what we had planned for elsewhere in Europe. Alan, our family's omnivorous reader, was our instant source of information about this or that tourist destination, and we drew on him as we adjusted and curtailed our plans.

When at last we were rolling in the pretty, light-tan wagon, it was a tight fit. In front, we improvised a third place between the two seats. Behind these was a single seat for three. That left two of our eight to accommodate themselves in the third section, facing backward, chins on knees, while sitting on the floor. Physically we were all adults or near it, with Larry, our *bambino*, as one inspector called him, having turned thirteen. But no-one complained. We were so happy to be on the road. We could rotate positions, taking turns, and there were few long drives.

Part of our daily routine came to be the lunch stops. They were not in elegant restaurants. Even dinners would usually be in a *trattoria* or other economically-priced eatery. For lunches we might look for a roadside stopping place, where we could lift the rear hatch-back and spread out bread, cheese, lunch meats, jam, and whatever fresh vegetables and fruit the local markets were offering. *Europe on Five Dollars a Day* was then a popular book. We didn't quite manage that daily limit; but at the end of our month, when I added up the expense of food and lodging, it proudly showed that for eight people we had held the cost, in US dollars, at just under six per person per day.

My recollection doesn't hold many specifically memorable scenes, and this is not intended as a travelogue. There was, for me, a discovery in Paris of Sainte Chapelle, a cathedral of light. Because it is not on a prominent height like Sacre Coeur, or strikingly situated on a river island, like Notre Dame, I found myself inside it almost unexpectedly captivated and awed by delicate stonework and glass that soared in pulsing light. This was not so much magnificent, as just beautifully bright.

Then we were in Rome. It was August and hot—all of those massive stones—although relieved by splashing fountains. But there was an evening when we sat at tables in an open *trattoria* at one side of a broad pavement. The openness gave perspective as, beyond it, gaunt and impassive in the evening air, rose the huge, timeless shape of the Colosseum. There it was—really, actually there!

We all remember one final episode of this trip. When, ending in Luxembourg, we were approaching the airport, a large plane was just taking off. It turned out to be ours. There had been a mix-up of information and we were left stranded. The Icelandic officials seemed appropriately concerned, particularly as they were confronted by a family of eight. To our relief, they managed to squeeze us into the next flight, scattered here and there as enough seats could be found.

When we arrived in New York, and as soon as I could find a pay phone, I called my sister, Elsie. I wanted to know about Mother. My concern was that we knew she wasn't well. Shortly before we were to leave for Europe, I had a trip to the West Coast and was able to stop by Westminster Gardens to see her. I found that she'd been moved to a small room in the nursing section. She was having problems with her arthritis and, more seriously, with her heart.

Very concerned, I told Mother that we could postpone our month-long trip, but she said, "No; you have planned this with all your family, and you need to go. They will take care of me here, as they are doing."

I hold strongly in my mind a picture as, leaving her and going down the corridor, I looked back, at the corner. She had come to the door of her room, wrapped in her dressing gown, and stood looking after me. I waved, although I doubted, with the weakness of her vision, that she could see that, and I didn't want to call out to her. She looked so frail, almost diaphanous. That was, I thought, perhaps the last that I might see her.

Elsie, with her travel business, told me that she would keep in touch with Mother, and, as we moved around Europe, she would leave at the American Express offices a message for me, as needed. There had been no adverse message at any stop. Heidelberg was the last, before our return flight; but time had been short there, and I thought that, with news having been all right and our flight home coming the following day, I could skip hunting up and inquiring at that last American Express agency. Now, at New York's Kennedy Airport, I had Elsie on the phone:

"Didn't you get my message? I left it at American Express in Heidelberg; you should have gotten it. Mother died day before yesterday."

There may have been more. I don't know. I went back to the family, in that huge, impersonal space, and Martha saw it in my face. She didn't ask me if I knew any details. I did tell her that there was to be a simple memorial service, as they did it at Westminster Gardens, and she said that I should go. All of the family drew around me, even while also it seemed that just I was there. Mother was gone, my mother, and I was there.

It was hard to realize the change. Of course, it had been years since I had seen her, or Dad, very often or for very long. She had not had recently a large part in my life. But now she was gone. That was the powerful, overshadowing fact my spirit must receive, accept, and go on. I felt no grief—just the finality of that change.

Elsie met me for the service at Westminster Gardens. I spoke about Mother. I recalled one painting that she loved, Raphael's "Madonna of the Chair," a small copy of which used to hang in their bedroom in Taegu. On our trip we had seen the original in the Pitti Palace in Florence, Italy—full size and in a broad, brilliant gold frame. I would not press the analogy, certainly not as some kind of sacred sign. It just spoke to me of Mother's love of art, of a beautiful human creation, and how by God's grace she herself had been transformed to share God's unimagined glory.

At Westminster Gardens Elsie and I also faced the task of taking care of the possessions that Mother had left behind. There were a couple of items that Elsie said she would like to have, and she would have them sent to her home in Nashville. For now, she must catch a flight back. The remaining personal things would not include anything she could use; so, since I had a longer time there, by a few hours, would I be willing to sort those things through? I said I would.

Again, of that scene, there is one moment in my memory. It was getting late. I sat in a patio with a table and a large trash can. Mother's papers and small items she had kept with her in her room were in a basket beside me. The basket was nearly empty when, reaching in, I drew out Mother's pair of reading glasses. They had rather thick, heavy lenses, made of glass, not plastic. I saw the nose pads and knew how they had pressed on the sides of her nose, leaving deep, red marks, and how she had sometimes wished there were some other way for her to see without that weight.

I looked for a long moment at those glasses. They had been so personal, so necessary to her, and at times painful. Shouldn't I keep them, I wondered—wrap them up and keep them with me for remembrance? I looked at the heavy lenses, almost inclined to run my finger gently over them. No, I wouldn't. I held them over the lid of the trash can, and I dropped them out of sight.

18

"Have You Thought About High School Teaching?"

FOR SIX YEARS WE were a middle-class, suburban American family of the late 1960s and early seventies. Then, again, the comfortable chair was yanked from under me. The Presbyterian Church (USA) decided to consolidate its agencies in New York City, meaning transfer of the Board of Christian Education and elimination of a good many positions, including mine. What to do now?

I thought that I might try for a return to college teaching, and began to put out feelers to smaller, church-related colleges where I might stand a chance, in spite of my rather hodge-podge resumé. But this was 1973. The economy was weak; college enrollments were down; and smaller schools were letting people go, not looking at untried candidates such as I.

One possibility did emerge—just one. Jamestown College, a Presbyterian school in Jamestown, North Dakota, expressed interest. Would I come out for an interview?

Yes, I certainly would. I flew out, finishing my trip in a rather small plane. The land flowing beneath my window was wide and flat. Few roads appeared and few, scattered settlements. There was water, but in occasional, rounded ponds, making me think of water hazards on a vast golf course.

When we reached Jamestown, I was cordially met by the college president, who took me through the town, then up a rise to the campus. On the way, I was struck by the larger-than-life figure of a steer, commandingly erected on a ridge. The campus, while modest, appeared attractive enough. Naturally, it was empty, as this was early summer.

The president had arranged, as part of my interview, for me to conduct a practice, one-on-one teaching session, with his daughter, currently a college junior, as my single student. I chose to discuss Matthew Arnold's poem "Dover Beach." The daughter was pleasant and responsive, and I felt good about the trial session.

I was hosted that night in the president's home, and we discussed salary. He said that he could meet my basic figure by appointing me to be Dean of Fine Arts, as well as an English professor. I heard about the community—and the North Dakota winter. The downtown stores had hitchingposts, where one could plug in a heating coil to keep his or her car's motor from freezing while purchases were made inside. Plainly, this would be a very different kind of life.

I flew home feeling ready to try it. The college president and his family had made it seem appealing—a place where I could establish myself and make a real contribution, and there would be plenty of opportunity for Martha as well.

But when I laid it out as well as I could to her, she said, "No, not possible." Our two youngest, Alan and Larry, who were still at home, backed her up. There was no way they could think of moving to such a remote location. I had to write to the Jamestown College president and regretfully decline.

*****

Providentially, three years earlier, on an impulse, I had done something novel and out of character. I had run for the Cherry Hill school board. Helped by the many contacts Martha was making in her church music, by a conspicuous sign mounted on the roof of our small car, and by our kids, who drove the car around and distributed campaign flyers, I was elected.

My three-year term meant many board sessions, during which I formed a close association with Robert Holl, the Cherry Hill school superintendent. At this juncture, Holl knew my situation, and he asked, one day,

"Have you thought about high school teaching?"

"Frankly," I said, "at this point I'm ready to think about anything."

The result? Within days, Martha and I were enrolled at Glassboro State College in southern New Jersey, taking education courses in its summer session to secure teacher certification, she in music K–12 and I in high

"Have You Thought About High School Teaching?"

school English. She said that if I were going into public school teaching, she would, too. The weather was hot; the schedule and the commuting, intensive; but our motivation was strong.

Cherry Hill had two large high schools: Cherry Hill High School East and Cherry Hill High School West. In English, there were teaching vacancies, but there was also a roster of candidates, with thirteen ahead of me. As weeks dragged by, the list was shrinking, places were being filled, but the start of school was looming closer. It was near the end of August—just days until classes would begin—before I finally had the happy news that I was hired.

From my first day, the experience was transforming. I was to be at Cherry Hill West. As I walked the halls, I was a public employee, receiving a public salary check. All of my working life, I had been related to the Presbyterian Church, whether working abroad in Latin America, teaching under Presbyterian auspices in Texas and Alabama, or organizing seminars and outreach efforts from my Christian education office in Philadelphia. I had been supported by contributions made to the church. Now, for the first time, I was in secular work, supervised and paid for by an agency of the State of New Jersey. My mind, my sense of obligation, felt somehow liberated.

Reception by my new colleagues was at first a bit restrained. I was in my fifties, holding a doctorate in English, yet I was a novice, without their experience in high school teaching. Add to that, I was an ordained minister, with whatever connotations that might have for some of them. And, finally, I had just come off the school board, which carried some overtones of friction and antagonism. Barbara O'Breza, chair of the English Department, must have felt puzzled, if not downright concerned, about where and how to place this new teacher whom headquarters had hired and passed along to her. For my part, I was very happy to be there, anxious to keep a low profile and to fit in.

A curious twist regarding my former school board membership: late that same fall the local chapter of the New Jersey Education Association (NJEA), of which I now proudly carried a member card, called us out on strike. I walked picket lines, devised my own placard to wear, and gathered with several others in early morning at one of the elementary schools, nursing a cup of hot coffee in the shivering chill, while we tried to dissuade anyone from entering the building.

Those events had a special value for me. They confirmed a solidarity with my new colleagues in our common cause. A strike was a rare happening in Cherry Hill, and there were some harsh confrontations. I was careful to avoid any direct clash, and much relieved when a settlement was reached, and we could get back to work.

There were about a dozen teachers in the English Department at Cherry Hill West, as I recall, two of whom, Joe and Lorie Truitt, became a generous and kind support to me. They were a husband-wife team, working in quite different areas.

I am remembering one early incident in my first year. I had a sophomore section that included some rowdy and rebellious students. English, quite reasonably, was a required course in all four high school years. This guaranteed full classrooms for us; but it meant that our students were there whether they wanted to be or not. Some chose to make it clear that they'd rather not.

One day a particular student made some insolent remarks near the end of the class period and started toward the door. I confronted him and backed him against a wall. I believe I didn't actually put my hands on him, and just then the bell rang, ending the period and our confrontation. But I was angry. Although the anger drained away, I was badly shaken, and I sat down in the quickly emptying classroom. A few moments later, Lorie Truitt came in and took a chair beside me.

"Some of the students told me," she said.

"What might I have done?" I asked. "How could I lose control like that?'

Lorie calmed and reassured me. After these years, I still gratefully recall that reassurance. There were other provocations, but there was not another such incident for me in my thirteen years at Cherry Hill High School West.

After the first year or two, I found a niche teaching Sophomore Honors. At the time, our department's pattern, particularly for the honors classes, was to focus reading for the sophomore year on world literature; then American in junior year and British in senior. The world literature required using translations where necessary and offered a wide-open field for selecting course materials. One of my favorite selections, for its depth and simplicity, came to be Hermann Hesse's *Siddhartha*.

I accepted an extra task, distributing our department's supply of books, as they were needed and were finished with, according to what each

"Have You Thought About High School Teaching?"

class was reading. Shelves in the basement comprised a sort of bookroom, where a row of each title had its place. My job was to keep track of these and carry on my shoulder a modest stack as requested by my colleagues, then retrieving those that had been used. There was satisfaction in having my domain in the cool basement and in keeping track of our department's book supply. A greater satisfaction came from being in touch with my colleagues and offering them a simple, personal service.

Joe Truitt was probably the best teacher that we had. His senior honors classes on British literature represented a climactic finish for many graduates of Cherry Hill West. One year I had a chance to collaborate with Joe in a memorable contest. A local television station put on a "Knowledge Bowl," inviting high schools throughout southern New Jersey to compete. Joe and I set out to recruit and train a team from West. We worked diligently, selecting the best volunteers and drilling them to be quick and accurate in their responses to a wide variety of knowledge questions at their high school level.

The competition was organized as an elimination tournament, and we easily won a couple of matches. But the deciding duel that loomed, as we knew it would, was to be with our arch-rival, Cherry Hill East. Their school was larger than ours, located on the more privileged side of the township, and tended to defeat us in every sports event. Routinely, they sent more graduates to more elite colleges and universities than we did; but we resolved that this time it would be different.

Our team went into the match well prepared. Joe and I watched through the sound-proof glass, hearing perfectly as our kids faltered a bit, and then began to beat the East students to the buzzer time after time. It was a wonderful, exhilarating, fulfilling thing—to beat East, and to beat them at academic information, brain power, in a Knowledge Bowl. Unfortunately, the competition was staged that one year only. Our one win had to be enough.

Martha, during this period, began teaching music in elementary schools. When there was an opening, she moved to Cherry Hill High School East. It was the newer as well as larger school and growing. Working with singing groups, both within the curriculum and outside it, Martha was doing what she enjoyed and did best. In her later years there, she directed single-handedly the student choruses and after-school groups of East's superb vocal music program.

In my spare time, I had begun a writing project. Bringing together my keen interest in the New Testament Gospels, my love of language, and a desire to attempt something major in poetry, I set out to tell, imaginatively, how the Gospel of Luke, the most beautifully written of the four Gospels, came to be composed.

Launched on the project and wishing I could give it more time, I decided to retire from teaching. I was sixty-seven and could retire with sufficient Social Security and pension benefits. Martha, three-and-a-half years younger, declared that she would retire, too. We would start this new phase together.

At school, in those final days, I was completely surprised and deeply touched when, in my free period, a student came to tell me that Mr. Truitt needed me in his classroom. I went along, a bit puzzled. When we got there and I opened the door, there was an instantaneous burst of bright streamers and applause. This was Joe Truitt's senior honors class, with many students who had been in my similar sophomore class two years earlier. One of them had made a poster with a large, cartoon-style, ink portrait of me, and they had covered it with notes of good wishes and their signatures. It was a high point of my high-school teaching years, along with another high point, when my English department colleagues held a festive farewell luncheon for me at a delightful, stream-side restaurant in a nearby town. For that occasion, I wrote and read aloud a whimsical parody on Thomas Coleridge's "Rime of an Ancient Mariner."

Those thirteen years of high school teaching were richly rewarding. I enjoyed the association with young minds—some of them very bright and curious. I came to appreciate the routine, even if teaching English involved wading through entire lakes of student papers. Also, there were the long, different, and useful summers.

19

Unexpected Call

SPRING EVENINGS CAN BE magical. For this one, the setting also was conducive. Martha and I sat under a white tent spread in the quadrangle of her alma mater, Westminster Choir College. Around the quad stood the American Colonial buildings that I had come to know and love, as I came to know and love Martha Bradway, that bewitching college sophomore, two-thirds of a lifetime ago. It was Westminster class reunion time. She was engaged in animated conversation with other college graduates. I could let my memory range back over a long span of years. This place held a rich trove of meaning for us, although our home was an hour's drive away and we had been retired from teaching for seven years.

Then Martha was tugging my sleeve. "Don, here are Eleanor and Stan. They live in a place called Rossmoor, just twelve miles away, and they have an idea for us."

What unfolded was quite simple. Rossmoor was a large, over-fifty-five community and they were active there in the ecumenical Rossmoor Community Church, which currently was without a pastor. Wouldn't we like to consider moving to Rossmoor—if I put my name in as a candidate and if the church called me to be its pastor? The community was pleasant, and the position was part-time, not too demanding.

Suddenly, on that evening—in the setting of that remembered place, its associations with our personal, lifetime commitments—a new, intriguing opportunity was opening up. This was how it had been before: God's Spirit giving a distinct, if unexpected, prompt.

All Stan and Eleanor needed from us was a nod. Stan disappeared to find a phone—no cell phones, then—and presently came back. If we could go to Rossmoor the next day—no commitment on either part, just to explore the possibility—Bill Tipper, a church council member, would be happy to meet us and show us around. Our two friends would have done that, but they had a promise to meet Eleanor's family in Philadelphia.

Bill Tipper, next morning, immediately became a friend. He deftly laid out the attractive aspects of Rossmoor, a thriving adult community of about 3,500 "senior citizens," built around the perimeter of a nine-hole golf course. He showed us the Meeting House, a pleasing building looking just like it stood in a New England village, which served flexibly for community gatherings and for worship by the Jewish congregation and the ecumenical Community Church.

We came away from our Rossmoor visit favorably impressed, finding, as we talked about it, that both of us felt ready for a change to such a place. The next day I called Bill and told him that.

At the time, Martha and I were living in Voorhees, a township neighboring Cherry Hill. On Sundays we were serving, on an interim basis, a little country church at a place called Janvier, about forty minutes deeper into southern New Jersey. She was at the small, balky organ and I in the pulpit.

On the second Sunday after our Rossmoor visit, as we were getting ready to begin our service, four visitors came in. A couple of the Janvier people knew about Rossmoor and immediately surmised where the visitors were from and why they were there. It was an accepted practice for a vacant church to send out a scouting team to hear a prospective pastor in his or her own setting.

For us, that was a bitter-sweet encounter. We were glad for the visit and the prospect it represented, but felt a nostalgic tug from the small, homey Janvier congregation. We made our choice, though, when the Rossmoor Community Church soon issued a formal call.

*****

Here again was a new experience for me, now at age seventy-four. I had a congregation of around one hundred fifty, most of them retired and all of them senior adults. Wholly absent were children, Sunday School, youth groups, and infant baptisms; and marriages were very rare. It was an ecumenical congregation, meaning no tie to any denomination or larger church organization, and no ecclesiastical tradition. The congregation elected the members of a church council, which had complete authority over church matters.

In time, I came to appreciate that autonomy. For example, we had quite a few members who, because of age or physical disability, were not able to attend services. They particularly missed the quarterly Communion Service. I could not take the sacrament to all of them at home, one by one. My Presbyterian church order required that the Bread and Cup be administered by ordained clergy, with only a rare exception to be made. But now I had an autonomous, ecumenical congregation.

I devised a plan, and secured the council's consent, for selection and confirmation of "pastoral elders." These volunteers, duly instructed, would work in pairs. Each team would have a short list of home-bound members to whom it would regularly take the sacrament, using a simple, reverent ritual that I adapted for them. There were parts for two leaders, and they would alternate in taking those parts as they carried, in portable form, the Communion bread and unfermented wine.

The response was excellent. The church members receiving this attention, regularly and warmly given, were grateful, and the pastoral elders found a glad fulfillment in the sacred act entrusted to them and a service they could perform. I was grateful that the task of ministry was being shared and that it was meaningful, both for isolated, home-bound members and for the pastoral elders themselves.

There was a different and earlier issue that became acute but turned out productively. Quite soon after we arrived in Rossmoor, the church organist decided to move away. Martha offered herself for the position, and the council confirmed her. The instrument then available in the Meeting House was an early-style Hammond electronic organ, not always responsive and distinctly limited in volume and in tonal variations. We soon began to wish and dream for something better.

Some exploration showed that a Hammond 36 could be purchased and fully installed for around $35,000. This organ had tremendous power, delivered through two large speaker units strategically installed. It also had a wonderful range of voices, including a sound drawer that could be drawn out, offering a selection of some fifty distinct settings. They could reproduce exactly the sound of some of the great organs of Europe, or of a Steinway grand piano, or of a chorus of human voices singing without discernible speech.

Martha and I thought that we could launch a campaign to raise the money for a Hammond 36. Installed in the Meeting House, it would benefit the Jewish congregation as well as our church and would be available to the community at large for concerts and special events. Initially, though, I had to secure council approval.

Immediately, there was concern. The church's budget, modest as it was—including only a part-time pastor—was chronically under-subscribed. If people gave to an organ campaign, they would give even less to the church, itself. That argument, put forward by some council members, was countered by others, who agreed with my belief that interest in a much better organ fund might stimulate general interest in, and dedication to, the church.

Discussion grew vigorous, even impassioned. One member, Ed, declared flamboyantly that approval of this measure would be given only over his dead body—as if things were going to get violent. In the end, with members evenly divided for and against, the council chair cast his deciding vote approving our organ campaign.

We went to work at the fundraising, using such devices as a large chart picturing a pipe organ. The electronic Hammond has no pipes, but, no matter. This way we could sell individual "pipes," marking progress and encouraging specific gifts. Our goal was the $35,000 figure. The campaign found generous support in the Jewish congregation and, more widely, in the community. In the end we had reached $40,000—enough for extras, such as that wonderful sound drawer with its fifty extra voices.

With approval by the Rossmoor management, the Hammond installers cut openings in the front wall of the Meeting House auditorium, one on each side of the proscenium, making them match exactly the clean, simple lines of its New England style. There, behind porous fabric screens, they installed the powerful speaker units. The result was a rich, even sound of the organ's voices filling the whole space of the auditorium.

I had a second-floor office in the front section of the building, from which I could easily cross to the auditorium balcony. One day, when Martha was practicing, I called down to ask her to play a favorite hymn.

"Now try some different stops," I called again.

She tested several and blended them.

"That's great!" She looked far away, where she sat at the console at the other end of the auditorium. "Now open it up all the way. That's a great hymn. Let me hear how it sounds up here."

Unexpected Call

She did just that, and the powerful, wonderful sound filled the whole space, every fissure. It shook the walls. It shook me, where I stood, down to the soles of my feet. I gripped a balcony rail, my knuckles going white, as the magnificent melody rolled around me:

> God of our life, through all the circling years
> We trust in Thee.
> In all the past, through all our hopes and fears,
> Thy hand we see . . .

The hymn—its words written by Hugh Thompson Kerr in 1916—is not widely known; but it has special meaning in my family tradition. Martha knew that, the way she let the organ speak. Now she reduced the volume, softening the effect, and I knew she was following the words.

> With each new day, when morning lifts the veil,
> We own Thy mercies, Lord which never fail.

"Beautiful!" I called down. "Now the third stanza, with a different setting."

There was a pause, while she chose some other stops, then the organ's voice again, more poignant.

> God of the coming years, through paths unknown
> We follow Thee.
> When we are strong, Lord, leave us not alone;
> Our Refuge be.

And now Martha added that special sound, a chorus of human voices joining in, without words. The words were in Kerr's hymn text, though, and deeply marked in my memory.

> Be Thou in life for us our daily Bread,
> Our heart's true Home, when all our years have sped.

I couldn't speak. Martha was closing the organ now. I went to close my office and go down the stairs to meet her in the foyer and hold her close, seeing her eyes wet, like mine. This was a rich, late phase of our life together.

*****

On January 7, 1999, my eightieth birthday passed. A month or so later I had some bleeding, and the diagnosis was bladder cancer. A urologist in Princeton assured me that the tumor was superficial. He had a non-invasive surgical procedure to remove it easily and definitively. I was glad to accept that, and to have his assurance, later, that he had taken care of it.

Meanwhile, I was discussing retirement with Martha. She gladly agreed, and so I asked the council chair for an opportunity to speak at the next meeting. He was my neighbor and close friend, Chuck Foster, now serving another term chairing the council. It had been Chuck who cast that deciding vote, five years earlier, to approve our campaign for the new organ. Chuck told me afterward that he didn't want me to speak now, because he guessed what I was going to say.

Let me put in here that Ed, the council member who so dramatically opposed the organ campaign proposal with his "over my dead body" declaration, later became a pastoral elder and actually teamed up with me, driving some distance from Rossmoor to take Communion to a church member, aged and unwell, who was in a nursing home, where she later died. He continued to be a cordial friend, until he, also, passed away.

Now I agreed with Council that I would serve until the end of June, allowing several months for them to begin the search for a new pastor. Martha announced that at the same time she would relinquish her post at the organ. Our Rossmoor Community Church friends gave us an eloquent send-off, including the gift of beautifully hand-lettered and hand-decorated certificates of appreciation, one for each. It was a send-off from service, although we planned to stay on in the community.

The six years as pastor of this unusual senior congregation had been rewarding. I became used to making hospital visits, and a little more adept than at first. They required driving back and forth the dozen miles to Princeton. That first fall the colors were particularly vivid. I took great delight in them, perhaps because in memory my mind still saw those barren hills of the north Chilean desert, above Antofagasta.

An aspect of our ministry—Martha's and mine—came to be the production of chancel dramas, chiefly for Christmas, several successive years. I wrote the plays, adapting them to our meetinghouse, and Martha supplied organ music for mood setting, background, and transitions—mostly just spontaneous improvisation. Our volunteer actors were all seniors, so we didn't expect memorization of lines. They were free to use cue cards. We only asked that, after a reasonable amount of rehearsing, they speak their parts to each other with natural feeling. Although the response from our audience/congregation was only good—not overwhelming—I enjoyed the challenge of writing these short plays and then producing them. Our most enthusiastic participant, as in almost all church activities, was Bill Tipper, the one who showed us around Rossmoor on that first day as a new-found friend.

The plays were meant to be timely in their message. One was presented when the inter-religious Serbian conflict was going on. It was laid in Srebrenica, and I made the couple seeking shelter, with the wife due to deliver her child, to be not Jewish, but Muslim—imposing that change on the Nativity story.

A play that was more ambitious, and for the Easter season rather than Christmas, was my *Passion 2000*. It takes place in contemporary Jerusalem, but in the home of two Palestinian-American sisters and their brother. They have moved there and become drawn to the charismatic Jewish teacher Yeshua (who does not appear on stage). These characters represent Mary (not the mother of Jesus), Martha and Lazarus, the trio in the New Testament who live in Bethany. We follow them, as the Passion story unfolds in a modern setting. Yeshua is assassinated, not crucified, but the outline of the Passion story remains.

*****

Only weeks after my retirement, my bladder cancer was back, announcing itself by an unnerving, dark-red hemorrhage. The urologist in Princeton said that it had now invaded the bladder wall. Surgery would have to include removal of the bladder, leaving me with a tube to an external pouch that would have to be worn constantly. Was there an option?

"You can consult Dr. Faulkner at the Rutgers University Department of Urology in New Brunswick. He's the one who taught all of us."

Accompanied by some of my family, I did that. Dr. Faulkner said that he and his associates were using a drastic, somewhat experimental surgery. They removed the bladder and any dispensable organs that could become affected by the cancer. Then they took a piece of intestine and constructed a "neo-bladder," making all of the connections, so that it could function in a nearly normal way. Would I wish him to do that?

Perhaps so. I would explore a little further. With our son Larry, who lived in Baltimore, I went to inquire at Johns Hopkins Hospital. We found that their procedure would be the usual removal of the affected bladder, substituting an external pouch.

I went back to Dr. Faulkner and told him I was ready to proceed. The story of that surgery and its outcome has already been told in the Preface.

20

The Gradual, Total Eclipse

I LOOKED DOWN THE hall, where our bedroom door was open. We were going out to dinner, and Martha was getting ready. She must be done by this time. Sitting on the edge of the bed, she seemed to be ready, but not quite.

Then I went numb; a cold wave washing over me. She was all dressed but was trying to put on a pair of hose—over her shoes! That was a sign—the first sure sign to come along.

I went to her. "You don't really need these. You look fine," I said, trying to make light of it.

She smiled and let me take the hose and put them in a drawer. We spoke no more about it, as we went on out to dinner. In fact, as that early shadow of Alzheimer's disease began, very sporadically, to show again, there was no comment; no discussion. I consulted our family doctor, a kindly, well-experienced Filipino-American physician. He had us come for a visit and put Martha through a standard set of mental tests, confirming to me privately the almost-certain diagnosis. There was a medication that might be of some help, which he prescribed, and Martha began to take it. She made no objection, and I treated it as routine.

Many couples would have gone into this together, talking frankly about it and sharing, while one supported the other. We had always been close, and I now felt even closer; but for me, it wasn't in the nature of our relationship to discuss the diagnosis, or even to show that I noticed anything different about her.

The Gradual, Total Eclipse

Had there been an earlier indication that this might have been coming? Certainly, there had been stress for Martha some months before this, during the long hospitalization of my double surgery for bladder cancer. For those weeks the family rallied around, with particular help from daughters Sylvia and Marilyn. Sylvia's home was in Bethesda, Maryland, on the border with Washington, DC; while Marilyn was teaching reading in Voorhees, New Jersey, an hour and a half south of the hospital in New Brunswick.

One Sunday evening during that time, Sylvia was staying with Martha. Her occupation in Washington allowed her some flexibility, so that more than once she stayed all night with her mother. On this evening, after long hours at the hospital, they had returned to our house in Rossmoor and had some supper together. Sylvia needed to leave for her home, but Martha was upset. Sylvia tried to calm and reassure her, saying that she would stay until Martha went to bed to get some rest.

Rest seemed impossible. Martha was too anxious. She broke down in tears, eventually becoming almost hysterical. She was sure that I wasn't going to make it out of the hospital. I was surely dying there, and she was alone.

Sylvia felt she couldn't leave her mother in that state but had her own problem. The next morning was a Monday. She had an important meeting in Washington, and she had to be there. She got on the phone to sister Marilyn:

"Can you possibly come up here? I don't dare leave Mom alone, the way she is, but I've got to be at this meeting in the morning!"

Things were critical for Marilyn, too, with school having recently started. She was a reading specialist and students had to be tested, evaluated and placed. She had already gone to bed when Sylvia called.

Marilyn could hear her mother crying in the background. She got up, hastily dressed again, and went downstairs. In a few moments her car's lights were on, the garage door was opening, and she was on her way.

Well into the night, the two daughters changed shifts at our house in Rossmoor. Martha had exhausted herself and fallen into a fitful sleep. There were hushed greetings and exchange of information, and Sylvia was on the road to her own home, with dawn breaking before she reached the Washington area. Marilyn stayed with Martha until early morning, when she could leave her calmed and asleep, then join the rush hour traffic on the New Jersey Turnpike, heading south. She got to school, with no sleep or breakfast, but on time.

During the six weeks of my hospitalization, we in the family had no idea of Martha's illness. It was later that we wondered, in retrospect, if the strain and stress she was feeling might have darkened the Alzheimer's shadow. Certainly, it was not many months after I was home that those first noticeable signs of it appeared.

Among various images one can use to describe the gradual, inexorable progress of Alzheimer's, I find effective that of a solar eclipse, except that the advance of the encroaching shadow is far slower. For us, it was almost imperceptible—that darkening that began to inch across Martha's thought, reflection and reason, and the functioning of her brain.

I had heard of an inclination of Alzheimer's patients to wander aimlessly, which could be dangerous. I went into her handbag, at a time when she had left it on her dresser, to find and remove her car keys. She mostly left the driving to me but could have a sudden idea that she needed to go somewhere. That was one risk I could preempt, without making an issue of it.

Cooking was another concern. Perhaps it was good that Martha didn't seem to want to cook much. I chose to accept that, relying on prepared foods we could pick up at the supermarket. Over time, I also developed a first-name friendship with the genial hostess of a nearby, take-out Chinese restaurant. Martha didn't seem to notice any difference in our dining patterns.

We had a vacation house at the New Jersey shore, about an hour-and-a-half away. It had replaced a large property in Maryland that our family had enjoyed for twenty years, part of a community on an estuary of the upper Chesapeake Bay. We were just getting used to this new house. It was some blocks from the beach, but had a dock in back on a canal, part of a network linked to a bay and then the ocean. I had a kayak and planned to enjoy paddling on the canals.

I felt no concern yet about leaving Martha in the house for an hour or two—that is until, coming back on my second time out, I saw her holding onto a post and leaning out over the water to look for me. The water was not deep there, but the bottom shelved off steeply to ten or eleven feet. Martha had been swimming since her childhood. Still, the way she was now, I worried whether she might panic if she fell in. Even a faint prospect of that frightened me. Unless someone were with her, I wouldn't paddle again beyond a clear view of our dock.

One evening, we had gone down to the Shore house for the day and needed to be getting home. We had a pleasant bedroom in the house, comfortably furnished, but Martha rarely agreed to stay overnight. So, we started to leave, locking our door and going out into a brisk December evening. With the holiday season beginning, there were festive colored lights twinkling on several homes up and down the block. In our neighbors' house, to one side of ours, there were more than just festive lights and a large wreath on the front door. The windows were also full of light and a sound of voices.

We were getting in our car when Martha said, "That looks so inviting. Let's ring the bell and go in!"

I was nonplussed. I knew these neighbors only casually, from chance meetings in the street or along the fence between our back yards. But Martha was insistent, and her voice began to rise.

"All right," I said, "we'll just wish them a Merry Christmas."

With nervous misgiving, I pressed the bell. Our neighbor, a pleasant young woman, came to the door, and I explained, as well as I could, that Martha and I just wanted to greet them.

"Of course," she said. "Come in, please."

She ushered us back to a sitting room where several others were gathered. Our acquaintance was such that she wasn't even sure of names; but everyone was cordial, and the mood was festive. Our hostess pressed on us some holiday goodies spread on a side table. I noticed, and was grateful, that she seemed to realize Martha's problem.

As soon as I thought it reasonable, I moved to excuse ourselves, and our hostess helped it happen in a gracious way. With relief, I got Martha into the car, making a comment on the friendly and kind neighbors. She said nothing about it, as if the whole incident had been quite ordinary.

*****

For six years, from the time we became aware of it, Martha's Alzheimer's advanced. She was still able to function rather normally, but I realized that we should be looking for a situation such as a CCRC (Continuing Care Retirement Community). A natural choice would be near Marilyn, the only one of our children who had stayed in New Jersey. We investigated several places, but none seemed satisfactory.

Then Marilyn suggested that we might look at a place named Lions Gate. It had opened earlier that year. The advertising specified "Jewish tradition." Would we like that? We pondered it: why not?

"You won't like the kosher cooking," a couple of our kids said. We thought that would be all right. We had lived in various parts of the world and come to appreciate different sorts of cuisine. We'd go visit Lions Gate.

The initial impression was favorable. Everything was fresh and new. The pleasant marketing representative who showed us around had a deft touch. As we came to one room in the common area, she said, "This is the chapel of all faiths."

Of course, I liked that. And I liked Rabbi Eron, the personable chaplain whom we happened to meet in a hallway. He was, I thought, someone I could look forward to knowing better.

In brief order, we signed a contract and went home to Rossmoor to prepare our move.

The unit we had selected at Lions Gate was medium sized. It had a quite large dining/living room, a small kitchen, two bedrooms, and two bathrooms. We would use the smaller bedroom as a study and guestroom; my homebuilt bookshelves would cover an entire wall.

For this kind of move, there had to be downsizing. That could be upsetting to Martha. I did some quiet planning with the children. Our Rossmoor house had a very large, irregularly shaped dining/living room—large enough to accommodate both Martha's Steinway three-quarter grand piano and her three-manual Wurlitzer electric organ. Neither of those could fit now, where we were moving. The piano was old; we had bought it much used and rebuilt. A Steinway agency bought it back, just for the value of the case. Our daughter Donna, who teaches piano in Palo Alto, California, wanted the organ enough to pay to have it shipped.

Donna also wanted my desk. It is a massive piece, the top a finished slab of wood with carving around the edges and carved panels on the supports at each side. We had found it, along with two equally massive, tall bookcases, in an auction house in Santiago when we first went, as a young couple, to Chile. All three pieces, ingeniously built with joints and tenons, had been partially disassembled, then crated and shipped, for every move that we had made over 61 years since we first moved that set from Santiago to Antofagasta. In Chile, the seller told us that the heavy, ornately carved wood was *roble americano*, American oak; but a furniture restorer in New Jersey, to whom I took the desk when the top had dried and split, declared

The Gradual, Total Eclipse

that it was mahogany. Either way, I was sad to part with that desk, although I hadn't really used it much. I preferred to do my writing long-hand on a tablet in my lap, then copy it on a portable typewriter—later, a computer. Now I gave the desk to Donna, along with one of the bookcases. The other one we set in our Lions Gate living room, where it stands beside me as I write this.

Martha and I had accumulated a sizeable collection of vinyl "LP" (long-play) records. Now, we no longer listened to them; we had a CD player. But as I pulled the LPs out and stacked them on the floor, Martha became anxious and emotional.

"You can't throw those away," she objected, her voice rising. "They're important, all of them!"

It was true that there were, among them, several albums that had been recorded over the years by one or another of Martha's choirs. Those, we would certainly want to save. For the moment, though, I wouldn't upset Martha by attempting any sorting.

"That's all right," I said. "We'll just stack them all over here." Later, when she was busy elsewhere, I would cull out the few memorable recordings and discard the rest.

Some of our children, who were near enough in distance, helped a lot with the downsizing and the move. We all could see that for Martha it was a stressful experience. Even while she was picking things up, she would put them in the wrong boxes. It was a relief for all, when we had moved to the new setting, an unfamiliar location, but surrounded by furniture and all the things she knew and loved. For me, the best part was that Marilyn and her husband, Dale, were now exactly one mile away, as I measured it on my car's odometer, door-to-door.

In our new environs we discovered and came to enjoy the Old Paintworks Pond. It was a mile or so down the main road that ran past the Lions Gate property. The pond takes its name from a paint factory that once operated at one side of it. The factory is gone. At that time, some large warehouses remained, but were hidden by a dense and pleasant grove. All around the pond itself there was a firm, well-beaten path, a favorite for strollers and joggers. There were several platforms built out over the water, with inviting benches for rest and reflection, and the walk was well posted: No Swimming; No Bicycles; No Dogs Allowed.

Martha and I could drive to the ample parking area, then walk the circular path as far as we felt like walking, stopping to sit on a bench of one of the small jetties, opting for sun or shade according to the season.

There was a place where the path passed near the site of the former factory. A choice had been made to leave intact three square, brick chimneys, quite tall and standing close together. I found them quaint and artistically pleasing. Martha did not. For her, they held some kind of menace.

"No!" she said, "I don't like it!"

After that I took care not to remark on the quaintly shaped chimneys.

On the Lions Gate property there is also a pleasant path that encircles the developed area. At the back, it runs through a patch of woods shared in part with two neighboring establishments. Martha and I occasionally walked the path in our early time at Lions Gate, and I later pushed her around it in her wheelchair. The cool shade of the wooded stretch could be pleasing on a warm day, and in fall some of the leaves were particularly brilliant. But she would protest, even wanting at times to turn back.

"I don't like the woods," she would say.

They were hardly "woods," just a few pleasant trees giving a bit of shade; but to her the light shade could somehow be dark and ominous. Such was the effect of that ominous Alzheimer's shadow.

*****

A day came when I took Martha to a nearby beauty salon for a hair trim. Her hair was beautifully—even brilliantly—white, having turned so rather early. She was still walking quite well, but her attention would wander. I was speaking with the owner of the shop, who didn't notice that Martha had moved around behind her. She finished her remark to me and stepped back, directly against Martha, who fell sideways, full length, striking a fixed treatment chair as she went down.

We both bent over her. She seemed dazed, but unhurt. We gave her time, then encouraged her to sit up—which was when she cried out. The pain was obvious and severe. The proprietress agreed to call for help.

When the emergency team arrived, they had a carrier with two plates that could be slid in to meet beneath Martha's obviously fractured hip, so that she could be lifted and carried to the ambulance with minimal twisting and pain.

My recollection blurs details of the tense times that followed: hospital admission, confirmation of the injury, consent for a hip replacement, and

The Gradual, Total Eclipse

the surgery. Martha's physical health was good, and her recovery went well. Just the day after surgery, she was able to stand and to put full weight on that mended hip, which seemed miraculous. Quite contrary, but equally notable, were the effects of the entire trauma—her fall, surgery and hospitalization—on her Alzheimer's. She was pushed down the darkening road of her illness, as those who know the disease well would expect.

After the surgery Martha was transferred to a rehab facility, where she could receive therapy; then, two weeks later, to the Skilled Nursing division at Lions Gate. She could understand ideas, when simply expressed to her; but now anything like conversation was impossible. As I sat with her in her room in Skilled Nursing one evening, words came to me, and I wrote this lyric poem:

> So we'll talk no more, my love.
> The moon is almost down.
> Few words are left; none to express
> What we have shared of loveliness,
> Of swallows skimming grass at dusk
> And firefly sparks among the trees,
> Of organ music in a shadowy nave,
> One soft light only on your face and hands
> And whiteness of the keys.
>
> In our silence now I hold you, warm and dear,
> As always—hold you here, and yet not here—
> Your smile flickering on the edge of time,
> As you move deeper into the not-time,
> And I reach you less and less. Love, it's still you
> Making the passage gently, by degrees.
> I'll make it too, sometime—we still count time—
> And we will talk again, or need no words
> For perfect sharing, in God's harmony.

The reference to swallows and fireflies evokes our former vacation house in Maryland. The reference to organ music recalls my being with Martha as she practiced at night in a large, empty church.

*****

I was resolved to keep Martha with me in our apartment as long as I could. Since walking was difficult for her, we used a wheelchair when going outside and a vertical walker in the corridors, as when going down to dinner. I needed to help her some at the table, but our friends and neighbors in Lions Gate were always kind and understanding. Martha's warmth and lovely smile had won hearts, from our first arrival in the community.

Eventually, I needed help and contracted with an agency to send a home health aide for four hours in the morning and four more in the evening. Andrea and Paula were two who excelled, and who formed the closest, almost-family ties. We ordered and set up a hospital bed and a single bed for me, replacing our queen-sized one.

In making these changes and in many other ways, our family's support was invaluable. Daughter Donna made frequent flights from Palo Alto to be on hand. Sylvia drove back and forth from Bethesda, when she wasn't abroad on assignment with the United Nations. And in particular, I leaned on Marilyn and Dale, for errands and advice, as they were so near. Our three sons, Tom, Alan and Larry kept in touch constantly by e-mail; but their various situations made for less frequent visits.

There were whimsical moments. One evening when Martha was still walking, and Andrea was accompanying us to the dining room. She and I were explaining in a conversational manner where it was we were going. Martha suddenly looked up and asked, "Who's going to cook?"

There were also sporadic moods of resistance, alienation, even hostility. These were sometimes made more disturbing by hallucinations—troubled ideas about people or things that were "out there," beyond the doors and windows, and insistent demands that must somehow be attended to. Her words would come in snatches, blurred, hardly comprehensible.

Martha generally knew me, sometimes clinging to me. I was grateful for that. But one evening, clutching my hand with almost fierce affection, she kept saying, "Call! Can't you call?"

"Who do you want me to call?"

"Call Don. I need to talk to Don."

I dreaded the day when she would no longer know who I was for her.

*****

For three more years the shadow kept advancing. Through Dr. Overbeck, our family doctor at Lions Gate, a specialist in geriatrics, I made contact with the Samaritan hospice service, to receive regular visits. Martha was not able to be up now. Our aides, supplemented by hospice and by me, were caring for her in her hospital bed. It was November, and Marilyn took the initiative, in her effective way, to gather the family for Thanksgiving,

The Gradual, Total Eclipse

arranging it for Friday, rather than Thursday, because that worked better for travel plans.

So, on Friday, November 28, 2014, we were assembled in Marilyn and Dale's spacious dining and living area. Five of Martha's and my six children were there, with their three spouses, and most of the grandchildren. It was a happy, if subdued, Thanksgiving celebration.

Then came a call from Sylvia, who was at Lion's Gate with Martha. The hospice nurse had told us that the end would be near; now Sylvia thought it very close. I went quickly to Martha's bedside, and the others followed. Our bedroom was filled, our five children there, and as many of the rest as there was space for.

Martha's eyes were closed, her breathing slow. I held her hand and bent close, as the children were doing on her other side. Time passed—not very long. The room was quiet. Martha was not struggling, not gasping for air. Her breathing simply and gently stopped. The long eclipse was now total. Alzheimer's advance, blocking the intricate circuits of her brain across those fifteen years and more in its irresistible progression, had reached and shuttered the last centers of involuntary command, her breathing and her pulse. Life simply ceased.

We had arranged for the services of an experienced funeral company, on the recommendation of a pastor friend. Now one of its representatives, with whom I had spoken, quickly appeared with an assistant. On their quiet suggestion, we all left the bedroom, filling our living room. I think some of the children thoughtfully stood close to me, obstructing my view, as they talked in low voices. It was all right. Very shortly I had a glimpse, imperfectly, as the two men passed from the bedroom, out the front door, one behind the other, carrying like a long suitcase, a dark, uneven bag.

That was well, for me. Martha had been leaving me for years, "making the passage gently by degrees." Now it was complete—this tired, limp body become unimportant—somehow, almost alien. My spirit accepted easily that it should be taken away, delivered to a crematorium, some ashes to be returned weeks later in an attractive, blue cloisonné urn with an Oriental-motif. I would place it in a niche of my study's bookshelves.

*****

The Christmas and New Year holidays were coming. We wanted a memorial service for Martha that might measure up to her own standard of beauty blended with reverent meaning. It should be genuinely a service, a devotional act invoking Eternal God. There should be organ music of high quality, as she would have chosen. The natural site was Trinity Presbyterian Church in Cherry Hill. The sanctuary is beautiful, the organ excellent, and Martha was a member there. Her association with Trinity reached back to our family's first settlement in Cherry Hill in 1967, when she became the church's organist and director of music, a post she held for seven years.

We set the service for late January, allowing time after the holidays for family members to make their plans and arrange travel. Two busloads of our Lions Gate friends attended, as well as friends and former colleagues from Cherry Hill, Rossmoor and Janvier. I led the service, including a brief meditation, and was pleased to hear my friend and colleague Rabbi Lewis Eron speak about the contributions Martha had made to life at Lions Gate, although she was no longer her full self when we moved there. All six children spoke about their mother, each one highlighting a particular quality of her life, as a mother, a musician, and a leader and mentor to so many people.

At the close of the service, our family formed a choir to sing *a capella* the lovely and moving "Benediction" by Peter Lutkin. It was always full of meaning for Martha. Her spirit sang it with and in us, who loved her and whom she so loved.

I include here another poem to her, written at this time. The imagery of the beach, footprints, a far shore, and the rest is just that—images to evoke the Unimaginable.

> Here is the beach, as in moonlight, more felt than seen,
> And your hand yet in mine, or not, I still can feel,
> Warm and serene, the shaking gone. My love,
> You slipped away in the moonlit deep, your breath
> A gentle wisp, and this eternal sea,
> Full and strong, lifting and carrying you.

> I am content. Alone, now, on the beach,
> But with the far shore nearer, and your love
> Free now, and with Love blending. Let it be.
> And let those prints you left, down to the gentle
> Surge, withdraw and surge, be on my heart
> Printed in promise. We will walk again,
> Hand-in-hand, will run and frolic on
> The unimagined shore, where God is all,
> And all is God, beyond the eternal sea.

The Gradual, Total Eclipse

I am glad, in frequent remarks and messages with our children and grandchildren, to share vibrant memories of Martha. And occasionally, moving around in my study, near those bookshelves that fill one wall, I glance at that beautiful, blue-themed urn in its high niche.

It is not a ghoulish reminder. Martha is not there—only some ashes, a residue of the body she once inhabited. She is not "anywhere" of my place-and-time world. But I know the vital reality of her spirit, which, like my spirit, is not defined by some here-and-now. Just as these words, as I write them, are ink marks on paper, but more and other than that; so, the thought-signals speaking in my brain are other and more. My spirit is with her spirit—with and in the Spirit, pondered and loved, who is All.

21

Three-Digit Milestone

How have I been managing since I have been alone here in Apartment 248 of Lions Gate? Certainly, the alone-ness had been coming on over a considerable time, as those of you who have experienced the loss of a loved person to Alzheimer's disease know so well. Yet, while there is still a physical presence of the loved one, no matter how altered, there is not the alone-ness that comes when that presence finally is gone.

My children expected and understood this. They arranged right away for the hospital bed in our bedroom to be dismantled and taken away; and to replace the single bed I had been using, they bought me a new, full-size bed, complete with a dark blue skirt, quilted spread, and blue pillow covers. This was a symbolic statement that I was to be fully at home—just *I* now, in what had been *our* apartment.

Helping with the transition was Katie, our cat, who was still with me. Martha and I and our family were dog people, having a succession of large dogs, German Shepherds and Golden Retrievers, as our children were growing up. But a large dog would not be practicable in Lions Gate, so we adopted Katie, a pretty calico cat, for whom one of Marilyn's neighbors had to find a home. After Martha died, Katie was a comfort for me, and I kept her until she died from an untreatable condition. I felt I wanted to fill Katie's place soon, so Marilyn found a suitable adult cat at the animal orphanage. Her name was Tootsie—by surprising coincidence, the name of our small dog when I was growing up in Korea. Although Tootsie had been a stray,

Three-Digit Milestone

she adapted to me and her new home quickly, and her affectionate nature has made her my constant feline companion.

Each person, at such a time, may have her or his way to keep meaningfully occupied. I would stress the *meaningful* part. For me, there were two interests that helped to keep me looking and moving forward: painting and writing.

For the painting, I had been doing something with watercolors in recent years; for example, at the Bay House, our vacation place on the upper Chesapeake, in the late 1990s. Now, at Lions Gate, the generosity of Carol Gooberman was giving me fresh impulse. Carol, an accomplished artist, regularly came to visit her mother in the Skilled Nursing division, and she began to offer weekly an informal class in the art studio to several of us. I found this both enjoyable and therapeutic. I got involved with it as Martha was in her final decline, and I became even more involved, gradually moving from watercolor to oils, after she died.

Of broader perspective and much more absorbing interest was my writing. I have described in the Preface how this interest took hold. After several other books, I very much wanted to write Martha's story—her story as she had been in the fullness of her prime, and also the story of our struggle in the decline of her illness. The result came to be *Martha and I: Life, Love and Loss in Alzheimer's Shadow*. I took a risk, writing the two stories in alternating chapters. Chapter 1 starts with little Martha, a fascinating, bright, whimsical child; but chapter 2 recounts a first sign of Alzheimer's encroachment on Martha's mature, adult career. Toward the end, the two stories draw inevitably together. The book was published in 2013, the year before Martha's death.

In the year following my losing her, I devoted many hours to—and received a special benefit from—reworking and expanding a narrative of my father's medical missionary career in Korea. That is, "old Korea," as I call it, because it differed so greatly from either of the Koreas on today's divided peninsula. I have written above, in chapter 15, how some fifty-five years earlier, while our family was in Mexico City and my parents visited us, I worked with Dad and Mother on such a manuscript. Over the years, several times I went back to the project, and managed a fairly complete text, but was never satisfied with it. I put it aside some time in the 70s and all but forgot it. After the publication of *Martha and I*, I needed a new writing project. My daughter Sylvia surprised me one day, producing a carbon copy of my old typescript, which she found among papers she had squirreled away, and she encouraged me to have a go at reworking it. Naturally, my parents were long gone; but in a carton I had some photographs and copies of early documents—enough, along with memories from my own childhood, to complete the manuscript that we had begun so long ago. Finally, in 2016, it was published as *By Scalpel and Cross: A Missionary Doctor in Old Korea*.

That was followed, in the two succeeding years, by two small books of a more creative, fictional sort. In these, I gather a group of five people representing three generations. On the pattern of Plato's dialogues, they discuss, in each conversation, a topic of prime interest, putting forward their different ideas and interpretations, under the guidance of a senior member of the group. The first book emerged as I sat on my balcony on spring and summer mornings, feeling a spiritual prompting that seemed to flow spontaneously through my mind and onto paper. The first volume saw publication in 2017 as *Dialogues with Jay: On Life and Afterlife*.

In that book there are, at first, just three people: Don, the narrator, who is essentially I, and his friend Luc (Lucas). These two, as graduate students thirty years earlier, had spent a summer in New Hampshire building a log cabin. You have read about that, or where it came from, in chapter 8. They join an older friend, Jay, also foreshadowed in real life in chapter 8. The group is subsequently rounded out by Luc's daughter, Beth, and her boyfriend, Ian. They come together in the CCRC (Continuing Care Retirement Community) where Jay, some thirty years older than Luc and Don, is living.

I use different venues for successive dialogues, including the edge of a delightful pond in the woods that Beth and Ian know and, because I love sailboats, the roomy cockpit of Luc's handsome sloop. Appropriate to the book's theme, however, the last of six dialogues has the group back in Jay's room at the Athens CCRC (named with the city of Plato's Socrates in mind), where Jay's health is faltering—such that in a one-page epilogue the other four of the group assemble in Luc's house to toast, appropriately, Jay's life, now ended, and what he had meant to them.

Since I had found this dialogue pattern congenial, I thought I would try a sequel. I would keep the spiritual orientation but set sharply against it some of the critical situations one might confront in today's world. As I had taken Jay out of the group at the end of my first book, I created Jennifer, introduced to Don by Luc, as "Jen, a younger friend of Jay," to which she adds, with a laugh,

"Not so much younger, but proud to be associated with his name in any way I can."

This book, while written as a sequel was also meant to stand on its own, so that a reader would not need to have seen *Jay*. The themes are suggested by the full title, *Dialogues with Jen: On Issues of Daily Living*. Jen is a retired English teacher, living alone. As the title indicates, in this book I imagine happenings, some of them very personal and stark, that involve members of the group, and about which they talk together.

For me, in this writing the creative, imaginative element has been stimulating. As also, the demand that I sort out my own ideas about some of the issues I am putting forward for my characters—and readers—to ponder. That has been, I suppose, my spiritual therapy. *Dialogues with Jen* was published in 2018, and now, in 2019, I press toward completion of this present book. In my best writing hours, I find my mind, my whole mental energy, so engrossed that I am too likely to lose track of time and place, forgetting my other needs and commitments. Yet, I'm grateful for that—grateful that by God's grace my hundred-year-old brain is capable of that kind of focus.

Which means that I am grateful for Lions Gate, the place where I live—for an assured daily rhythm. This includes an early dinner each evening with a few friends and such activities as my oil painting, Canasta games (I've re-learned the game that friends and I sometimes played many years ago), and community programs, among which is an occasional concert by fine young classical musicians. For the last of those, I have been active from the beginning in helping to organize a committee—we now call it the Lions Gate Classical Music Guild—that raises funds among our residents and works with an outside agency to plan the concerts and to bring the talented artists to our Commons Hall.

Moderation has been a rule for me throughout life, and it is definitely my pattern here at Lions Gate. To that I would add, prominently, keeping a positive, hopeful attitude toward life. I am grateful, also, for good health. This means gratitude for inherited genes and for the opportunity to maintain a healthful lifestyle, that includes swimming a mile a week. As I've been doing that for about eight years at Lions Gate, I calculate that, at fifty miles a year, I've logged some four hundred miles in our fifteen-yard pool.

*****

In May of 2018 the Presbytery of West Jersey recognized the seventy-fifth anniversary of my ordination to the Ministry of Word and Sacrament, as we call it in the Presbyterian Church (USA). The warmth and personal character of this simple recognition ceremony was arranged, typically, by Debby—the Reverend Doctor Deborah Brincivalli—in her role as Executive Presbyter, which includes being a sort of "pastor to pastors," as she cared for all of the ministers in her presbytery.

It was in May 1943, in a moving ceremony in Bethlehem Presbyterian, that country church in northwestern New Jersey, where I, a soon-to-graduate theological student, knelt down, and felt the hands of ministers of that presbytery laid on my head and shoulders in sign of my ordination. In our Presbyterian system, ordained ministers are not members of any local congregation, but of a presbytery, which is their nurturing and supervising body.

Now, after my seventy-five years of service in South and Central America, in Texas, Alabama and New Jersey, the presbytery of West Jersey, my current spiritual home, was attesting to it with a beautiful, framed certificate. I hung it on a wall close to my computer screen, where I see it daily, remembering and giving thanks to God.

*****

As my remaining days or years unfold, however that may prove to be, I treasure the loving support of my children and grandchildren and extended family. Daughter Marilyn and my son-in-law Dale, just five minutes away, are a particular source of counsel and reassurance. My weekly dinner and long evening in their home is always refreshing, as is Marilyn's bright voice on the telephone, or at my door when she brings me groceries or whatever else she has thought of for my well-being.

Donna, Martha's and my firstborn, comes to see me surprisingly often, despite the cross-country trip that requires. She joined Marilyn, Dale, and me on a cruise to Alaska, and as I write this is scheduled to do so again, cruising to Cuba. Her loving support is always in reach.

My daughter Sylvia has been an invaluable help with my writing and publishing projects, and in my morale. Although her home is two-and-a-half hours away and she is, at times, on overseas assignments, she is periodically my house guest, using the convertible sofa in my den. We also consult back and forth by email, and I value every input.

Three-Digit Milestone

All of Martha's and my six children, their spouses and their children, stay in close touch through email and at special times, like my hundredth birthday. For that occasion, my children planned and carried through a gala celebration here at Lions Gate. They created and distributed widely a beautiful invitation that included a photo I liked for the bright sweater that it showed and for a stretch of ocean water behind me. The entire family came to the party—even my two-year-old great grandson Jack and his parents from near Boston, and Sylvia, all the way from Myanmar, traveling thirty hours each way. Only one of my grandsons couldn't make it. My nephews Bob and Don, two of my brother Arch's five sons, came with their spouses; Billy and Dave Caldwell, sister Elsie's sons, flew in from Tennessee and North Carolina with their spouses, which was very special. With a large turnout of my fellow Lions Gate residents and many friends from outside, we had about a hundred and twenty filling our Commons Hall with warmth and good wishes.

*****

I know that I've been blessed. I have had less than a usual share, it seems to me, of pain—both physical and emotional—of disappointment, grief, and bereavement. While there have been upheavals, abrupt turnings in the road, and a great trial with the loss of Martha, there has always been an assurance, by God's grace, of a way forward.

Quite naturally, as I have passed a milestone marked "100" on that road, I have been reflecting more on where and how it ends. As to the "where," that is a word that we use here and now, in our space/time reality. My faith-conviction is that in death we emerge, or leave behind, space and time. I am using language of space/time, because that's all we have here, for now. Faith affirms some kind of entrance, by God's grace, into a transcendent reality, which is unimagined. The only images we could use to try to imagine and describe it would be of our present reality, and therefore totally unsuitable and inadequate.

What I do affirm by faith, standing on that affirmation, is that beyond that transition, beyond the end of this present life, there is justice, cleansing, and there is joy. How is the twisted and distorted made straight—the harsh evils of our abuse of one another purged—washed out and left clean? God knows, and only God.

Let it be enough that I affirm, by faith, that when I die, I do not cease to be. The essential being—the soul or spirit that is I—is yet real, more real than I have known it in this life. I affirm this for my beloved Martha, who went on ahead of me. I affirm it for all humanity in all human existence, under the wisdom and purpose, the righteousness and holiness of transcendent God.

This is all we know—all that we are created to be able to know—and it is enough. It opens out to Glory. My eyes, the eyes of my mind, dazzle. They can see no further. This is Joy—Transcendent Joy—sublimating my passing of the boundary of mortal life.

Illustrations

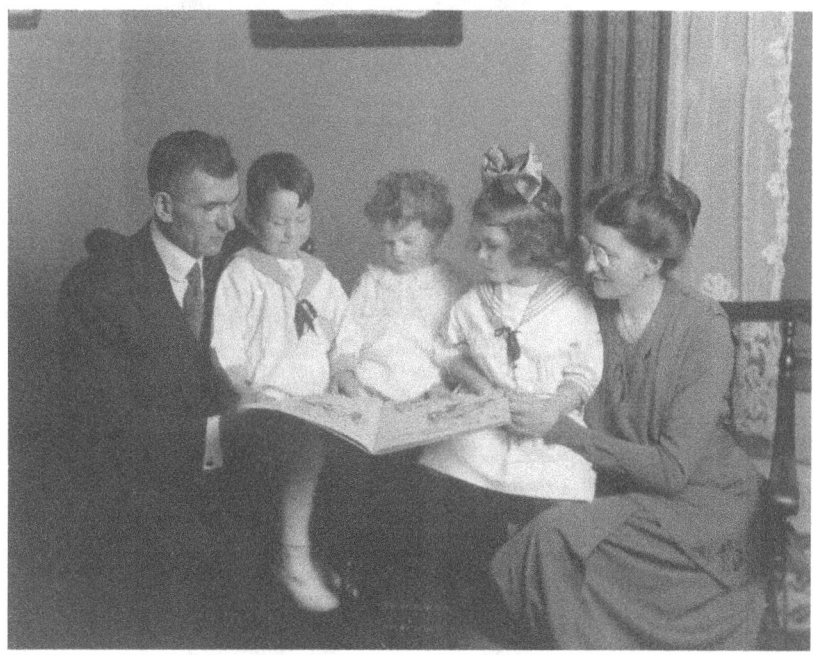

Photo 01. Family portrait with Don, age one: Archibald G. and Jessie Rodgers Fletcher and children Archie, Don, and Elsie, 1920

Photo 02. Senior year at Pyongyang Foreign School, 1935

Photo 03. Martha and Don, dressed for a formal concert at Westminster Choir College, 1943

Photo 04. Studio portrait of Don and Martha as new missionaries, 1945

Photo 05. Don leading a youth group on the Antofagasta shore, 1950

Photo 06. In the pulpit of the Iglesia Presbiteriana Cristo Rey, Antofagasta, 1953

Photo 07. Portrait of Don, age 42, 1961

Photo 08. Martha and Don in Cherry Hill, 1987

Photo 09. Family celebration of Martha's and Don's 50th Wedding Anniversary, 1992

Photo 10. The family at Martha's Memorial Service, 2015

Photo 11. Portrait of Don, age 97, 2016

Photo 12. Don with his six children, celebrating his 100th birthday, 2019

Photo 13. Don still preaching at age 100, 2019

Other Works by Donald R. Fletcher

I, Lucas, Wrote the Book (Xlibris, Philadelphia, 2003): a fictionalized account, based on biblical scholarship, of the writing of the Gospel of Luke

View from the Playroom Floor (Xlibris, Philadelphia, 2004): a series of philosophical- theological essays offering a world-view from where we are, like children absorbed with our toys

Turnings: Lyric Poems Along a Road (Outskirts Press, Denver, 2009): a memoir of a spiritual journey that includes a selection of poems written over the course of a lifetime to express faith and feelings

The Gift: Looking to Jesus as He Was (Amazon CreateSpace, 2010): a pondering of the words and acts of Jesus in the Synoptic Gospels to approach Him as He was

Martha and I: Life, Love and Loss in Alzheimer's Shadow (Wipf and Stock Publishers, Eugene, OR, republished 2019): a love story that chronicles the author and his wife's experience with Alzheimer's disease, and a portrait of her life as a musician, wife and mother

By Scalpel and Cross, A Missionary Doctor in Old Korea (Resource Publications, Wipf and Stock Publishers, Eugene, OR, 2016): a non-fiction story of a Presbyterian medical missionary told against the background of Korea in the first half of the 20th century

Dialogues with Jay: On Life and Afterlife (Resource Publications, Wipf and Stock Publishers, Eugene, OR, 2017): patterned roughly after Plato,

Other Works by Donald R. Fletcher

dialogues of five people sharing their thoughts on an afterlife beyond the boundaries of space and time.

Dialogues with Jen, On Issues of Daily Living (Resource Publications, Wipf and Stock Publishers, Eugene, OR, 2018): five friends, representing three generations, get together to discuss contemporary topics, patterned after Plato's dialogues.

www.ingramcontent.com/pod-product-compliance
Lightning Source LLC
Chambersburg PA
CBHW050812160426
43192CB00010B/1726